Minority Business Success

Minority Business Success

Refocusing on the American Dream

Leonard Greenhalgh
and James H. Lowry

STANFORD BUSINESS BOOKS
An Imprint of Stanford University Press,
Stanford, California

Stanford University Press
Stanford, California

©2011 by the Board of Trustees of the Leland Stanford Junior University.
All rights reserved.

Special discounts for bulk quantities of Stanford Business Books are available to corporations, professional associations, and other organizations. For details and discount information, contact the special sales department of Stanford University Press. Tel: (650) 736-1782, Fax: (650) 736-1784

Printed in the United States of America on acid-free, archival-quality paper

Library of Congress Cataloging-in-Publication Data

Greenhalgh, Leonard.
    Minority business success : refocusing on the American dream / Leonard Greenhalgh and James H. Lowry.
        p. cm.
    Includes bibliographical references and index.
    ISBN 978-0-8047-7434-5 (cloth : alk. paper)—ISBN 978-0-8047-7435-2 (pbk. : alk. paper)
    1. Minority business enterprises—United States.   2. Success in business—United States.   I. Lowry, James H., 1939–   II. Title.
    HD2358.5.U6G74   2011
    338.6'4208900973—dc22

                                                                    2010036786

Typeset by Westchester Book Services in 10/15, Sabon.

This book is dedicated to the men and women of the civil rights movement who had the courage and determination to take enormous risks to create a different future for minorities and women.

CONTENTS

Preface   ix

Acknowledgments   xiii

1 *Minority Business Success Is a National Priority*   1

2 *To Succeed Is to Survive, Prosper, and*
   Grow to Scale   19

3 *Government Must Refocus on Inclusion*   50

4 *Corporations Should Refocus on Development,*
   Not Procurement   86

5 *Support Organizations Should Refocus on*
   Core Mission   112

6 *Minority Business Success Requires Leadership*
   and Direction   134

   Notes   165

   Index   171

We are at a turning point in history. A decade into the twenty-first century, the United States has changed; so has the world around us. We need to adjust to the new economic landscape we are seeing. That is what this book is about.

The end of 2008 saw the overleveraged U.S. financial system collapse, sending global financial markets into chaos. This precipitated a shakeout in vulnerable industries, with small-to-medium-size suppliers paying a heavy toll as their value chains atrophied.

But the end of 2008 saw us achieving some positive milestones too. For the first time in U.S. history, a minority was elected President, an accomplishment that would have been unimaginable four or five decades earlier. America seemed to wake up one morning to discover that it had truly become a multiethnic, multicultural country.

Barack Obama did not win the election because the minority proportion of the U.S. population had expanded to the point that they had enough votes to get "their man" elected. Obama's supporters spanned every demographic category. The country was ready for a minority President—or a woman President, had Hilary Clinton prevailed in the primary elections—because the country had accepted the ideal of America as the great melting pot, the land of opportunity, the country where all men and women are created equal and all American-born citizens can rise to the very top.

But the success of a few minorities at the very top of their domains should not distract us from the plight of the many. Minorities—and, for that matter, women—still struggle to overcome the vestiges of institutionalized discrimination that have been in place for centuries. As a result, the American Dream is real for some people but elusive for others; despite its egalitarian ideals, America has not always lived up to its own standards of decency and fairness. For most of its history, the United States has been dominated by white Anglo-Saxon Protestant (WASP) men who have discriminated against African Americans, Asians, Hispanics, Native Americans, and women. The legacy of that shameful aspect of American history has been the underparticipation of minorities and women in the U.S. economy. Today, that is a problem.

The problem is that although the United States is a big economy, it is rapidly becoming one of many able contestants in a highly competitive global business environment. The notion of national competitive advantage has never been more important, because whole industries can migrate overseas, seemingly overnight. The migration begins with an industry-leading American corporation sinking, perhaps due to its own complacency, but taking down with it the "industry cluster" of suppliers that successor corporations would need in order to take its place. When this happens, the wealth-generating capacity of that industry departs our economy too. Jobs disappear; revenue streams are lost; capital to reinvest dries up; and tax revenues vanish, leaving the country strapped for the cash it needs to upgrade its physical and intellectual infrastructure and to maintain the national standard of living and defense, security, and social services. It is a downward spiral.

So America needs all of its citizens making their best contributions to the country's economic well-being. Goods that are not made well here will be made offshore. Services that are not performed well here will be outsourced to countries that can do a better job. Innovations that are not successfully brought to market here will be developed elsewhere and sold here. We would become a consumer nation rather than a producer nation, our balance of payments would favor other countries, the dollar would be worth less, and our standard of living would decline. We are already seeing it happening. So it is time to change course.

This book is about enabling the full participation of minorities in the U.S. economy. We have no other choice, because minorities are well on their way to becoming the majority of our workforce and our entrepreneurial economy. But what we have to say about minorities is also applicable to women, who also have much to contribute. Women are already the majority, and they too are on an uphill journey to overcome the economic exclusion of past decades. But we will not go into detail about the unique situation and needs of women in this book. We will keep the main focus on minorities and deal with the unique challenges of women business owners in other works.

As we think about the economic inclusion of minorities, we need to take into account the context in which we must move forward. We can observe the wreckage of the real estate markets, the victims of the credit crisis, the increase in wealth of the wealthy and the decrease in purchasing power of the middle and working classes, the upheaval in the auto industry and manufacturing in general, the demise of the experiment in removing regulation from the markets, the acceleration of global climate change due to carbon emissions, the waning of religious conservative political influence in North America and its increase in the Middle East, and the realignment of geopolitical power and influence. Collectively, these observations should make us realize that the context of business has changed—irreversibly.

Yet in the midst of crisis, there is always opportunity. The U.S. government developed a set of economic stimulus programs designed to create jobs, boost disposable income, and elevate the country out of recession. The idea is for money to be spent so that money can be earned: that is the bottom line in stimulating the economy. It is well established that small business is the biggest source of job creation and wealth generation in the U.S. economy, so most of the money needs to end up in the hands of entrepreneurs. It is also well established that access to capital has always been more difficult for minorities and women. So an obvious way to channel funds to address the credit crisis is to make it easier for small businesses to get the loans they need to grow their businesses—which will allow them to give out more in wages and spend more on purchases.

But increasing access to capital without making sure the money will generate long-term revenue streams amounts to "throwing money at the problem," and we have squandered billions of dollars demonstrating how ineffective that tactic is. The emphasis needs to be on *development* of minority businesses, of which capitalization is just one element. Successful development involves a comprehensive, integrated set of interventions. Piecemeal solutions *have* never worked and *will* never work. That is why our efforts need to be refocused.

This book explores what it means to develop minority businesses so that they take their necessary place in the U.S. economy. We will see that in past decades, the primary emphasis has been on helping minorities gain access to supply chains. That is, advocates have created opportunities for minority businesses to compete for a small percentage of relatively unimportant outsourcing. In many cases, this has amounted to little more than issuing a purchase order and then hoping for the best. We will see that this approach does not measure up to global best-in-class purchasing strategy, in which the central objective is to work with high-potential suppliers and help them get better—in other words, to *develop* them.

We begin by showing how demographics are changing. We then trace the evolution of minority inclusion in the U.S. economy and explain the consequences of not addressing the challenges posed by changing demographics. Next we look at what minority firms need to be doing to take their place in the economy, because they are the most important element of the solution. Then we examine how governments, corporations, and support organizations ought to refocus their efforts to foster minority inclusion in value chains. Finally, we offer ten specific recommendations that will form the bedrock of a new paradigm for developing minority businesses—so that they can fully contribute to national competitive advantage.

We hope this book will inspire you to think differently about the role of minority businesses in the U.S. economy and what we as a nation ought to be doing to ensure their maximum contribution to our prosperity.

ACKNOWLEDGMENTS

This book represents the culmination of a program of research and intervention that spans more than 30 years of helping to create a different future for minorities and women in the U.S. economy. Over that time, many individuals have shaped our thinking and sharpened our insights. Without any implication that they share our conclusions, we owe a particular intellectual debt to the following people:

Punam Keller, Dave Pyke, Eric Johnson, Joe Hall, Rob Shumsky, Andrew Bernard, Matt Slaughter, Alva Taylor, Fred Wainwright, Lynn Foster-Johnson and Carolyn Clinton of the Tuck School; Daniel Heath of the White House; Ronald Langston, David Hinson, Efrain Gonzalez, Anita Cooke Wells, Ivonne Cunarro, Heyward Davenport, and Kay Bills of the Minority Business Development Agency; Karen Mills, Clara Pratte, LeAnne Delaney, Chad Moutray, Ying Lowery, Porter Montgomery, and Bill Elmore of the U.S. Small Business Administration; Reggie Layton of Johnson Controls; Michael Robinson and Marilyn Johnson of IBM; Bill Moon, Don McKneely, and Sharon Patterson of the Billion Dollar Roundtable; G. Winston Smith, of AT&T and Microsoft; Daryl Hodnett of Procter & Gamble; Wesley Stith of Clark Construction; Betsy Zeidman of the Miliken Foundation; Jethro Joseph of Chrysler; Earl Graves and Alan Hughes of *Black Enterprise*; Kenton Clarke of DiversityBusiness.com; Rob

Fairlie of the University of California, Santa Cruz; Chief James Ransom of the St. Regis Mohawk Tribe; Frank Venegas of the Ideal Group; J. Scott Bryant of MeadWestvaco; Louis Greene of the Michigan Minority Business Council; Don Chapman and Rick Wade of the Department of Commerce; Jack Stevens, Vic Christiansen, and Mike Luger of the Office of Energy and Economic Development, U.S. Department of the Interior; Benita Fortner of Raytheon; Bo Andersson and Diane Freeman of General Motors; Charles and Geoffrey Blackwell of the Chickasaw Nation; Ray Brice, Theresa Barrera, and Anthony Soto of Wal-Mart; Jothi Purushotaman and Anand Stanley of United Technologies; Clyde Gooden of NANA; Tony Brown, Ray Jensen, and Armando Ojeda of Ford Motor Company; Daryl Williams and Bob Litan of the Kauffman Foundation; Linda Denny and Susan Bari of the Women's Business Enterprise National Council; Kate Boyce of Patton Boggs; Jim Webb and Dana Hill of the St. Louis Minority Business Council; Margo Gray Proctor and Ron Solimon of the National Center for American Indian Enterprise Development; Harriet Michel and Steve Sims of the National Minority Supplier Development Council; Tony Dolphin of Springboard Technologies; Shelia Hill of the Chicago Minority Supplier Development Council; Wallace Ford of GoodWorks International; Emil Jones of the Illinois Senate; David Thomas and Jim Cash of Harvard Business School; George Fraser of Frasernet; Farad Ali of the North Carolina Institute of Minority Economic Development; Jerry Fulmer of Wisconsin Energy; Chief Chad Smith and Jay Calhoun of the Cherokee Nation; Fred McKinney of the Greater New England Minority Supplier Development Council; Ginger Conrad and Barbara Oliver of *MBE* Magazine; Bob Wallace of the Bith Group; Kermit Thomas of the Venture Fund Development Group; Don Graves of the Business Roundtable; Jeremiah Boyle of the Federal Reserve Bank of Chicago; Mike Bolger of the Asaba Group; Hank Wilfong of the National Association of Small Disadvantaged Business; Roger Campos of the Minority Business Roundtable; Jim O'Neal of Frito-Lay; Barron Harvey of Howard University; John Robinson of the National Minority Business Council; Carol Daugherty Foster of the Minority Hall of Fame; Timothy Bates of Wayne State University; William Pickard; Jose Arriola of Avanti; Parren Mitchell of the U.S. Congress; Richard Holland of Holland Advisors; Matt Krentz, Larry Shulman, Carl Stern, Joe Davis and Hans - Paul Buerkner of the Boston Consulting Group; Steve Reinemund of Wake Forrest School of Business; Don Jackson of Central City Production; Dipak Jain and Steve Rogers of the Kellogg School of Management, Northwestern University; David Perez and Samuel Boyd of the National Association of Investment Companies; Marc Morial of the National Urban League; Gene Tabor, Monetta Stephens and Adrienne Trimble of Toyota; Deborah Chapman; and many more

Final thanks are due to the thousands of minority, Native American, and women business owners and service-providers who over the years have shared their insights about the challenges they face and the solutions they have explored. Teaching is genuinely a two-way learning experience, and we have gleaned as much knowledge as we have imparted. It is a genuine privilege to work with this group of business leaders.

1   MINORITY BUSINESS SUCCESS IS A NATIONAL PRIORITY

EXECUTIVE SUMMARY

History repeats itself. Problems go unattended for years until the nation is forced to deal with a crisis. The launch of Sputnik shocked us out of our complacency about America's leadership in space. The publication of Rachel Carson's book *Silent Spring* made us aware that we had been poisoning and plundering our environment. The meltdown of the credit system revealed the underregulated banking system to be catastrophically overleveraged. What had been invisible to the public eye suddenly became visible.

The nation is on the brink of another crisis. Minorities are destined to become the major population group in the coming decades, but they have not been allowed to make their proportional contribution to the U.S. economy. Today we *need* their contribution, not only to speed economic recovery but also to boost the nation's output of goods and services to preserve our position in the increasingly competitive global marketplace.

Globalization has increased the importance of national competitive advantage. Wealth flows out of lackluster economies into the coffers of nations that do a better job of value creation. Understanding this, all industrialized countries—except, it seems, the United States—have a National Industrial Strategy that plans what must be produced domestically, which industries are strategically and economically important, and which policies and infrastructure must be in place to create, attract, annex, or retain the high-profit, high-growth industries.

A U.S. National Industrial Strategy would acknowledge the importance of minorities to America's economic future. When minorities become the majority of the workforce, the supply chains, and the entrepreneurial economy—as they must—their success in creating wealth will determine the fortunes of the nation and everybody within it.

To date, the odds have been stacked against minority economic success. We once denied minorities access to ballot boxes, lunch counters, and drinking fountains. Now we deny them access to good educational opportunities, capital, and all but token business opportunities. Minorities do not contribute to the U.S. economy in proportion to their representation in the U.S. population because they cannot. The motive to own successful businesses is strong enough, but many barriers remain intact.

This situation needs to change. The business case for minority inclusion is compelling. It has obvious implications for public policy, corporate outsourcing practices, and support organization efforts. But there has been little progress during the last two decades, even though the minority population has grown dramatically. We are using approaches designed for a different era and are not producing the results the country needs. We need to refocus those efforts. This book suggests an alternative paradigm that will create a different future for minorities in the U.S. economy.

MINORITY BUSINESS SUCCESS IS A NATIONAL PRIORITY

We have a national problem, but we lack a national strategy that is adequate to deal with it.

The national problem is the steady decline of national competitive advantage in the face of increasingly fierce competition from rival economies in Asia and Europe.

We saw symptoms of the problem emerge shortly after the new millennium began, in the form of rising unemployment, erosion of the value of the dollar against other currencies such as the euro, the export of somewhere between 25 million and 40 million U.S. jobs overseas, the increase in the balance of payments deficit into the trillion-dollar range, and the demise of U.S. prestige abroad. The country has been hamstrung by an outdated ideology that opposes planning and regulation—despite the obvious fact that we are operating in a global marketplace in which rival countries plan a concerted effort to take over lucrative U.S. industries and U.S. global market share.

It is time to rethink what is in the public interest. The so-called "free-market system" has created perverse incentives for business leaders to "take the money and run." Propounding the myth that markets are self-regulating, opportunists mastered tactics to drive up short-term stock prices and apparent profitability, and they rewarded themselves with handsome bonuses for doing so. Their freedom to skirt market regulation was abetted by politicians who were beholden to them because of the country's election-financing policies—an arrangement that misaligns self-interest and the public interest. But the system they created and exploited was simply not sustainable, as evidenced by its sudden collapse.

After those in power did, indeed, take the money and run, the taxpayer was left to pay the tab for restoring the vitality of the economy. But, as this book will point out, we cannot restore the economy and national competitive advantage without paying special attention to changing demographics and to the adequacy of the nation's human capital to compete effectively in the global economy. We urgently need a National Industrial Strategy that sustains the key industries of today and fledges the growth industries of tomorrow. The strategy needs to be inclusive, forward-thinking, and impactful in the short run—and sustainable in the long run.

We will see that a National Industrial Strategy involves identifying the industries we want to keep within the U.S. economy, ensuring adequate workforces to staff them, fostering the development of industry clusters and infrastructure to enhance their viability, and promoting the development of American-based value chains to ensure that they remain globally competitive. The free-market system of the past decade will not preserve or promote national competitive advantage; we need a well-thought-out plan for recovery and progress, a plan that is not distorted by lobbyists sacrificing the common good to favor special interests. As a nation, we will have to realign public policy, corporate strategy, and nongovernmental support in order to embark on a trajectory that holds more promise for our economic futures.

But before we propose a comprehensive solution, we need to understand the context of the problem facing the U.S. economy. Most importantly, we need to understand the magnitude of the demographic shift and its implications.

THE MINORITY POPULATION WILL SOON BECOME THE MAJORITY

For most of the twentieth century, white males dominated the U.S. workforce, the country's entrepreneurial economy, and the multitier supply chains that sustained U.S.-based major corporations. The future will be different. Before the middle of the twenty-first century, minorities and women will dominate the workforce, the entrepreneurial economy, and the complex value chains upon which corporate success now depends.

The nation's approach to fostering their inclusion was developed in the 1980s. The situation has changed, and our approach needs to change accordingly. We cannot afford to settle for anything less than a new paradigm that will integrate and refocus the efforts of corporations, public-sector agencies, and support organizations. And we need strong leadership to ensure that we are achieving the necessary level of impact.

The urgency arises because the demographic shift is momentous. *Minorities will soon become the national majority.* That is a fact. We are not speculating about what might happen based on a set of theoretical assumptions; we are talking about people who have already been born or have immigrated to the United States. Table 1.1 and Figures 1.1 and 1.2 show the data, based on information compiled by the U.S. Census Bureau[1] and related sources.

If you do not like reading data tables, then here are the important facts:

- There will be more minorities than whites in the U.S. population by 2042.
- Six of the country's eight largest cities are already minority dominated.

- Minorities—especially Hispanics—have significantly higher birth rates than whites.
- Immigration has boosted the minority population.
- The majority of today's children under five years old are minorities.
- The (primarily white) baby boomers are reaching retirement age and will be dropping out of the workforce and the entrepreneurial economy during the coming decade.
- Minorities have less accumulated wealth to pledge as collateral for business loans.
- During the past decade, while the rich have been getting richer, the lower middle class and the poor—where minorities are overrepresented—have been getting poorer.
- Minorities disproportionately get stuck in poverty cycles, leading to higher dropout, unemployment, and incarceration rates.
- Recessions harm minorities more than whites.

THE NATION IS UNPREPARED FOR THE DEMOGRAPHIC SHIFT

This country is not preparing for this unprecedented demographic shift that will affect economic recovery in the short run and national competitive advantage in the long run. The most pressing problem is that today's minorities—who are tomorrow's employees and suppliers—are not getting

TABLE 1.1

Percentage of U.S. Population in Each Racial Category, 2010–2050

Year	2010	2015	2020	2025	2030	2035	2040	2045	2050
Race									
White	65.0	62.9	60.7	58.5	56.3	54.1	51.9	49.7	47.6
Hispanic	15.8	17.4	19.0	20.6	22.3	24.1	25.8	27.6	29.2
Black	12.9	13.0	13.1	13.1	13.1	13.2	13.2	13.1	13.1
Asian	4.5	4.9	5.3	5.6	6.0	6.3	6.7	7.0	7.3
Multiracial	1.8	2.0	2.2	2.4	2.7	2.9	3.2	3.5	3.7
Native American	1.2	1.3	1.3	1.3	1.4	1.4	1.5	1.5	1.6

the education they need to staff the workforce in the service/knowl-
edge economy, or the help they need to fully participate in the entrepreneurial economy. This situation hurts minorities because it destines all
but a few of them to remain an economic underclass; it hurts the nation

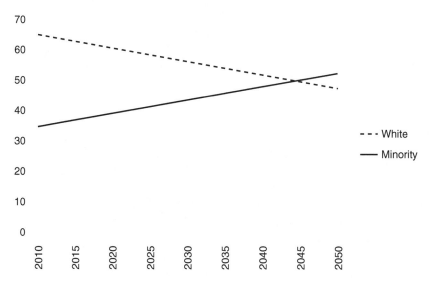

FIGURE 1.1
Percentage of Whites and Minorities in U. S. Population, 2010–2050

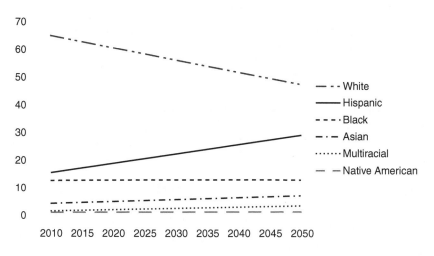

FIGURE 1.2
Percentage of U. S. Population in Each Racial Category, 2010–2050

because the economy can neither recover nor excel if half of the population is unable to make its full contribution to national prosperity.

In addition to the threat to our future prosperity, we have seen, throughout history, that when an economic underclass becomes the majority, the established order—with its institutionalized inequities—becomes unstable. The class division between the embarrassingly wealthy and the unacceptably poor becomes a *cause célèbre*, and revolt in its various forms awaits only a triggering event. In our lifetime, we have seen this happen in Paris, where mobs have roamed the streets burning cars, in Greece, where gangs of youths have fought police, and in the United States, where looting has spilled over from the inner cities.

We ought to pay attention to the lessons history can teach us. Sociologists point out that revolutions do not happen when people are down and out; they happen when there is hope that people's situations will improve. The downtrodden have higher expectations when their circumstances are improving and consequently less tolerance for the unfairness of their predicament. So apply this history lesson to the situation of an African American president being elected through a campaign of "Change We Can Believe In." What is likely to happen if there is no change and if the American Dream remains out of reach for so many? How will the status quo be tolerated by people who believe they have elected a president who ought to be highly aware of their plight? Few historians would predict complacency.

Overt conflict is an obvious cost of chronic hopelessness and despair. Alienation, seething resentment, and the depressed motivation to better oneself, pervasive in inner cities and poor rural areas, are the less obvious but more insidious costs. A community of people who do not see how they can get ahead in life and have given up trying is a drain on the economic system; the larger the community, the greater the negative consequences. So the demographic shift brings with it a simmering problem that is growing in magnitude each day.

A deeper problem is the adverse economic impact of minority underachievement. The highly educated and experienced baby boomers are beginning to retire en masse. They will need to be replaced in the U.S. workforce and the entrepreneurial economy. Demographic changes destine their replacements to be primarily minorities. If we do not foster minority inclusion and do everything we can to ensure their success, the impact will extend beyond the minority community to constrain gross domestic product and national affluence.

In practice, we are not really doing much to foster minority inclusion and success, despite having so much at stake. Unless we get focused on impact, instead of contributing robustly to the national economy, minorities will remain on the sidelines of their value chains, generating little wealth, few jobs, and low tax revenues. Instead of reaping the benefits of inclusion, the U.S. economy will have to divert public funds that could instead be invested in infrastructure, research and development, education, defense, or homeland security.

Thus the issue of minority inclusion is not about historically poor Americans becoming better off at the expense of the rich: it is about all Americans becoming progressively worse off than they were at the turn of the millennium. It is already happening: think how much your purchasing power has eroded since the year 2000.

We need to understand the major barriers to the economic inclusion of minorities—particularly in the case of African Americans[2] and Hispanics. These are:

- inadequate education;
- difficulties in securing funding for their businesses; and
- limited access to mainstream supply chain opportunities.

The long history of discrimination and neglect in this country has led to the present predicament. Let's look closely at each of these constraints.

POOR EDUCATIONAL PREPARATION LIMITS MINORITY ECONOMIC SUCCESS

We first need to look closely at the root cause of the economic underparticipation of minorities. Prior to the civil rights movement, exclusion was the result of institutionalized racial discrimination. Today, the hate-radio talk shows reveal that vestiges of that era remain among some right-wing extremists. But even in the absence of bias, many minorities cannot participate in the lucrative parts of value chains because minorities are not achieving the level of literacy—much less advanced education—necessary to contribute fully to the service/knowledge economy.

Let's be sure we understand what this terminology actually means. Up until a couple hundred years ago, the United States had a primarily agricultural economy, consisting of hundreds of thousands of farms employing farmhands. After the Industrial Revolution, manufacturing surpassed agriculture as the principal source of revenue and jobs in the U.S. economy. Factory workers did not need education any more than farm workers did, because both were performing thoughtless tasks. During the 1980s, services—white-collar jobs, health care, retail, insurance, information technology, and so on—had become more important than manufacturing. These jobs required a literate workforce. Today, the most profitable enterprises are in the knowledge economy, where value is created through innovation, intellectual property, analysis, or special know-how. Google, for example, is more profitable than the Yellow Pages because it is knowledge based rather than service based; for the same reason, a biotech firm will be more profitable than a nursing facility. Illiterate or marginally literate people cannot hold down lucrative jobs in the service/knowledge economy, so they have limited career choices and thus make up a large proportion of the unemployment rolls.

Inadequate education is a problem in a country where wealth depends on success in the service/knowledge economy. In most of this country's minority-dominated communities—inner cities, barrios, poor rural areas, and Indian reservations—*only about half of today's ninth graders will graduate from high school*. And many of those who graduate will not be fully able to read, write, do basic math, and use a computer—the most basic skills required for employment that involves more than supervised manual labor. The country already has an oversupply of unskilled labor. The undersupply of educated technical/professional workers is an increasingly critical issue.[3]

The low level of educational achievement in many minority-dominated communities sustains a tragic intergenerational *poverty cycle*. The cycle is initiated because a child's preschool experience determines his or her learning level in kindergarten and in every grade beyond. Let's contrast a household in an affluent suburb with a household in a poor inner city to understand the system dynamics that operate.

In the affluent household, educated parents provide the child with a broader vocabulary and are more likely to tune in to television channels that will foster the child's learning. In grade school, the affluent parents are better able to coach the child struggling with homework and to stress the importance of paying attention in class and doing homework diligently.

By contrast, in the inner-city household, the children of illiterate parents start kindergarten with a diminished vocabulary and little encouragement to do well in school. The poorly educated parents cannot help the child with homework, often because they cannot do it themselves. The child is "behind" in every grade level, with little help or support coming from the home environment or the neighborhood. Add in typical inner-city adversities—such as a local culture that disrespects educational achievement, few positive role models, fetal alcohol syndrome, poor nutrition, a history of abusive treatment, and unaddressed health problems— and the odds are really stacked against those children ever gaining an adequate education. Unusual inner-city children can rise above the lack of preparation and support they get in their home environment, but typical inner-city children find grade school an uphill challenge; many of them get discouraged and drop out. Earning ability is tied to educational achievement (see Figure 1.3[4]), so poverty in one generation tends to create poverty in the next.

These dynamics are unfolding in a U.S. educational system that itself has been eroding over the past few decades. The principal causes of this decline seem to be local funding of schools (poor communities get poorly funded schools), local control of curriculum (local politics can determine which subjects get taught and to what standard of achievement), poor retention of good teachers (average time before resignation is less than five years), and difficulty removing bad teachers (due to tenure, seniority systems, and union rules). Whatever the causes, the problem is severe. We should be ashamed that *the United States is the only industrialized nation in which young people are receiving a poorer education than their parents' generation received.*

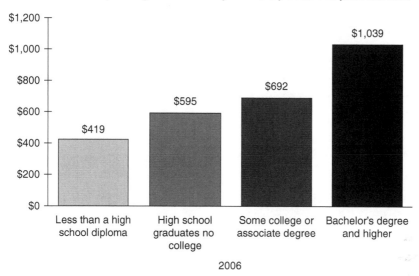

Median weekly earnings of full-time wage and salary workers 25 years and older

FIGURE I.3
Education Pays Source: Bureau of Labor Statistics

But more than ashamed, we should be alarmed. This is not only a local or state problem; it is also a national problem. The United States needs a highly educated workforce to maintain national competitive advantage in the global economy. The country also needs a growing infusion of knowledge-based new ventures to energize and sustain the entrepreneurial economy—and to replace major corporations that have become complacent and lost their technological or competitive edge.

Here is the bottom line. Despite the growing needs in the service/knowledge economy, minorities as a group are not getting the education the country needs them to have, nor are their entrepreneurial enterprises getting the help they need to survive, prosper, grow to scale, and take their place in the economic system.[5] It is sad if jobs are going overseas because of labor costs. It is a national tragedy if jobs are going overseas because our expanding minority population lacks the basic literacy to do those jobs. And that tragedy is unfolding before our very eyes.

CHRONIC UNDERCAPITALIZATION INHIBITS
MINORITY BUSINESS ENTERPRISE ACHIEVEMENT

Aspiring entrepreneurs from well-off white families have several options for acquiring start-up or working capital. They can use inherited money, borrow from family members, or get family and friends to cosign their notes; they have homes that can be used to obtain a second mortgage, or other assets that can be pledged as collateral; and they may even have social relationships that connect them to bankers and create positive predispositions to grant loans.

Aspiring entrepreneurs from typical minority families have fewer options. *The net worth of a minority family is about one-tenth the net worth of the average white family.*[6] So borrowing significant amounts of money from family and friends is unlikely to be a realistic option. Minorities are more likely than their white counterparts to rent rather than own their residences, so taking out a second mortgage is seldom a source of low-interest capital. And they rarely have interconnected social relationships with bank lending officers, who tend to be white.

Now add to this picture the well-documented tendency—perhaps subliminal—of some white bankers to stereotype minorities as greater risks. It may not happen in a particular case, but it happens often enough that minorities (and women, for that matter) end up with a higher cost of credit than a white male applicant would pay.[7] And this was true before the recent tightening of the credit markets due to the mortgage-industry scandal.

FIRST-GENERATION ENTREPRENEURS NEED
GUIDANCE AND SUPPORT

The country needs a thriving minority entrepreneurial economy. But entrepreneurship cannot be learned in school as easily as can other occupations, because the knowledge and judgment needed to be a successful entrepreneur will depend on the type of business involved. A retailer's challenges, for example, are very different from those facing a software developer, a high-tech manufacturer, or a trucking company.

Certainly there are some business concepts and principles that are best learned in a traditional academic format. But much of what an entrepreneur needs to know is specific to a particular niche, and this is where good guidance can save the entrepreneur from an ulcer or ruin. Think about how Jewish entrepreneurs have traditionally learned to operate in New York City's Garment District. They have fathers, uncles, aunts, neighbors, and friends in the business, all offering advice (whether solicited or not!). Similarly, many Cuban Americans in South Florida are from families who are all entrepreneurs, and young people learn how to run a business from daily dinner conversations and family gatherings, so that by the time they reach adulthood, they are steeped in the entrepreneurial culture. And Southeast Asian immigrants might know the fishing business as a result of generations of experience in the old country before settling in the U.S. Gulf states. In all of these cases, the success of entrepreneurs is fostered by guidance and support from family or the community.

Now contrast the case of minorities who have the entrepreneurial spirit but have not been immersed in an entrepreneurial environment: examples might be Mexican Americans who came to the country as agricultural workers or African Americans whose ancestors were brought in to work on plantations and whose families have always been farm or factory workers. How do they pick up the contextual knowledge that cannot be learned from textbooks or classes?

Finding a mentor or coach can be very helpful to such first-generation entrepreneurs, but many minorities are not included in the social networks of white-dominated industries such as the construction trades, advertising, or finance. If we want minority businesses to succeed, we need to foster networking opportunities where people who face analogous challenges can draw on each other's experiences and make connections to people who can lead them to opportunities. We cannot afford to wait for existing networks to become more inclusive, nor can we expect minority business owners to do the reaching out: entrepreneurs have a tendency to be self-reliant—that is why they chose to be entrepreneurs rather than someone else's employee. So we need to go beyond providing access to the knowledge that can be gained from instruction and also facilitate the development of insights and skills. In short, we need to focus on minority business enterprise (MBE) *development* in the broad sense of the term.

IT IS IN THE PUBLIC INTEREST TO ENHANCE MBE SUCCESS

Having specified what we need to do, it is time to remind ourselves why it is so important to do it.

A National Industrial Strategy involves identifying the industries the nation needs to retain or develop, making sure there are adequate workforces to staff them, fostering the development of industry clusters and infrastructure to ensure their viability, and ensuring that American-based value chains are globally competitive.

The strategy needs to take into account the changing demographics. In the twenty-first century, minorities will come to dominate the workforce, the entrepreneurial economy, and the complex value chains upon which corporate success will continue to depend. This leads us to an important guiding principle: *The United States cannot restore its national competitive advantages unless it fosters the survival, prosperity, and growth to scale of its minority businesses.*

More specifically, half of the U.S. working population and half of the country's entrepreneurs will soon be minorities. They obviously need to be successful if the United States is going to be successful: we cannot be globally competitive if half of our economy is underperforming.

Let's review these relevant facts:

- The highly experienced, well-educated baby boomers are reaching retirement age, leaving many companies operating in the all-important knowledge economy desperately short of qualified personnel.

- The American educational system is turning out 70,000 engineers, scientists, and technical professionals a year; India is turning out 350,000; and China is turning out 650,000. These are approximations, but the relative orders of magnitude are informative.

- 51 percent of U.S. master's degrees and 66 percent of U.S. doctoral degrees are earned by foreign students, many of whom leave the country soon after earning their degrees, often because of visa restrictions.

- A motive for global outsourcing is to take advantage of higher literacy rates overseas as well as lower labor costs.

- Global outsourcing has resulted in somewhere between 25 million and 40 million U.S. jobs being "exported."

- When important work is outsourced abroad, host countries set up indigenous industries to compete with the company doing the outsourcing. Examples include software, automobiles, aircraft, and consumer goods.

- Global outsourcing has benefited the richest 5 percent of Americans but has left the poorest 50 percent worse off economically.

- The United States is the only industrialized nation that lacks a coherent National Industrial Strategy that would influence which industries we foster and which industries we protect. A symptom of the policy vacuum is the demise of the U.S. manufacturing base.

- Over the past decade, U.S. immigration policy has primarily fostered family reunification, while the rest of the industrialized world has shaped immigration policy to build human capital in order to enhance national competitive advantage.

- Modern industries are integrated supply chains, not self-sufficient, vertically integrated corporations. Their viability depends on the competitiveness of the "industry cluster" of industry-specific suppliers and the "infrastructure" of suppliers that enable the local economy to function.

- When half of the U.S. population is minority, half of the supply chain will need to be minority owned and operated. The success of major industries will be determined by the excellence of the industry clusters and infrastructure upon which their major companies depend.

- The supply chain is dynamic. Many of yesterday's major suppliers have already gone out of business, and many of today's major suppliers have lost their competitive edge. Tomorrow's prosperity depends on how innovative, responsive, and lean are tomorrow's suppliers.

- The failure rate of entrepreneurial businesses is higher for minorities than for white-owned ventures.

- Small business is the largest source of job creation in the U.S. economy.

- Minority-owned firms tend to hire more minorities than do white-owned firms.
- The larger the minority firm, the greater the minority job creation.

This mosaic of facts portrays the current predicament of the United States. The country's place in the global economy has been steadily declining as we have lost competitive advantage against rival nations. Indeed, we have already ceded whole industries to Asian countries, and more industries are targeted for takeover. To make matters worse, we have to deal with an economic crisis that is acknowledged to be the worst recession since the Great Depression. And the two wars and the staggering budget deficit have left this country with few resources to spare in crafting solutions to America's predicament.

It is time for action. We cannot move forward with a strategy that leaves half of our economic engine idling: it needs to be firing on all cylinders. That means we need to get minorities (as well as women, of course) fully involved in the business mainstream.

More specifically, unless we unleash the potential of the minority population, the past success of the U.S. economy—and the unprecedented wealth it has bestowed on U.S. residents—cannot be sustained in the coming decades. This means not only will minorities continue to be denied a fair share of wealth and opportunity, but all Americans will also face a bleaker future. Whites entering their careers will have decreased opportunity as the competitive advantage of U.S. corporations erodes in the global economy and the spending power of U.S. workers shrinks. Mid-career whites will continue to experience a plateau or an erosion of their standard of living. And whites approaching the end of their careers will be disappointed in the yields of their equity-based pension plans, which depend heavily on the success of large U.S. corporations with global reach. Look around you. It is already happening.

This is not a case of minorities prospering at the expense of whites: in fact, our economic models show that minorities will not be significantly better off than they are today.[8] Their standard of living will remain stagnant, while whites' standard of living will decline. Therefore, the situation is not win-lose: it is lose-lose. That is why it is in the public interest to enhance MBE success. We need to embark on a new trajectory and create a different future.

IT IS TIME TO TAKE ACTION

In the 1960s, the heroes of the civil rights movement led this country out of institutionalized discrimination in the social and political realms. *In the new century, institutionalized discrimination is primarily economic.* Minorities can sit at lunch counters, use the same toilets, and vote, but they continue to underparticipate in the entrepreneurial and mainstream economies. This form of discrimination is institutionalized in the sense that *the system* stacks the odds against their success.

Everyone pays a price—the privileged as well as the expanding underclass—when minorities and their communities cannot achieve economic self-sufficiency, much less the prosperity that would lift them out of their intergenerational poverty cycle.

In the ensuing chapters, we will pinpoint what has been holding minorities back and how they should be taking responsibility for their own progress; we will identify promising industries and value-chain roles; we will show how corporations, governments, and support organizations can be more effective in promoting minority inclusion; and we will challenge leaders in the supplier diversity movement to collaborate and innovate in devising a comprehensive solution.

Our goal is to call forth everyone's best efforts to move beyond today's supplier diversity practices and to make a greater impact. Critics view the supplier diversity movement to have become a supplier diversity *establishment*—implying complacency, territoriality, and stagnation. Without doubting the sincerity and commitment of supplier diversity professionals, it is fair to note that our supplier diversity practices have changed very little over the past three decades, while the world around us has changed radically.

Change induces entrenchment among those who are threatened by it. It induces innovation and adaptation among those who are inspired by the possibilities. We need leadership to emerge that will rejoice in what we have accomplished to date but not settle for the status quo, because the people who pay the price are not only the minorities who could be better served but also the country.

This book will show that we are facing a multifaceted challenge that requires an integrated, multifaceted solution. It will also become obvious that the fragmented approach we have been using to date will not earn the level of public and corporate support that is needed to take us beyond where we are today.

The problem of minority underparticipation is complex, and inescapable: it calls for efforts to be refocused so that they achieve real impact; it calls for nothing short of a new paradigm of intervention. It is a national priority.

The chapters that follow explain what could be achieved and what needs to be achieved.

2

TO SUCCEED IS TO SURVIVE, PROSPER, AND GROW TO SCALE

EXECUTIVE SUMMARY

Minority-owned businesses need to fully contribute to the U.S. economy because our national prosperity depends on it. But minority success has been inhibited by a long history of discrimination—in its overt, subtle, and institutional forms. As a result, minorities' rates of business ownership, their accumulation of wealth, and their economic contributions have been depressed.

There is no shortage of entrepreneurial aspirations in the minority community. Like their majority counterparts, about one person out of ten wants to be a business owner rather than to work for someone else. But the would-be entrepreneur must traverse steep inclines on the pathway from aspirations to achievements: the uphill challenges are start-up, surviving, prospering, and growing to scale.

Most start-ups are destined to fail—either being poorly conceived or poorly managed. But even those that do not fail at the outset need to survive competition and economic fluctuations. The necessary condition for survival is to create real value for customers, which involves articulating a compelling value proposition and delivering on it.

To prosper, and not merely survive, minority business enterprises (MBEs) need to play an important role in value chains, which means they must be strategically focused and proactive. MBEs who are passive—who wait for an RFP (request for proposal) to cross their desks, or who deal in "commodity" services or products set aside to achieve diversity-spend targets—are unlikely to prosper. They will take on roles that are peripheral to major value chains, and they will come up against hordes of diverse competitors desperately underbidding each other, driving down profit margins.

Wealth creation by MBEs is good for the nation. It reduces economic dependency, increases tax revenues, creates jobs for minorities, provides positive role models, breaks the cycle of poverty that fuels intergenerational underachievement, and nourishes the local economy through the multiplier effect. But the greatest positive impact comes when that wealth is reinvested to grow the minority business to scale.

MBE growth is required for participation in the value chains of major organizations. Size facilitates the economies of scale that are necessary in the context of global competition. Size has also become a prerequisite for doing business with major corporations due to supply-base consolidation. Major corporations cannot absorb the inefficiencies of dealing with a large number of small suppliers—they need to deal with a small number of large suppliers; therefore, minority-owned businesses must grow in order to remain eligible for this important outsourcing business.

The changes required to evolve from a small start-up to a major supplier are not linear: they are transformational. Thus a large business is not a small business with a lot of employees added: it is qualitatively different. When entrepreneurs outgrow the face-to-face organization that took them through the start-up phase, they have to delegate the day-to-day management of the company to professional managers. When the organization becomes a medium-size business, the owner's role goes beyond delegation to creating a complex structure that will achieve tactical results. When the business is large, the owner is yet another step removed from it, focusing on strategy rather than tactics, setting targets and keeping track of progress through reports, and managing relationships with customers, suppliers, bankers, regulators, and the community.

There are three strategic options for achieving the necessary scale: organic growth, acquisition, and strategic alliance. Organic growth involves adding sales volume and, as volume increases, adding work-processing capacity and people to staff and manage the expanding enterprise. Organic growth is slow, it places demands on cash flows, and it stalls when the business outgrows its structure and requires transformation. Acquisition is a shortcut: in essence, the MBE buys the increased capacity rather than grows it. Strategic alliances are collaborative arrangements that can provide the benefits of scale. None of these approaches is without hazards, but scale must be achieved if minorities are ever going to fulfill their role in the U.S. economy.

As a nation, we need minority businesses to succeed; therefore, we need to enable their survival, growth, and prosperity. Enabling creates a fourth option for achieving scale: large corporations can stand up a business for a qualified minority top management team to own and run. The stand-up can be a spinoff of an existing corporate subunit, an acquisition of an existing supply business, or a creation of a new value-chain partner. This is becoming a promising option because as more and more minorities are granted access to the ranks of management, they are gaining the experience to run a strategic business unit; the skill set needed to run a large supplier business is very much the same. Alternatively, high-potential MBEs can be enabled to roll up a set of smaller competitors to become a larger-scale supplier. The challenge of obtaining acquisition capital will be eased by the higher probability that corporations will do business with the scaled-up MBE.

Minority business owners must do their part, of course, but enabling is warranted because the system has been inhibiting minorities' full participation for centuries, with vestiges of that shameful era still persisting. Enabling involves giving minorities a fair chance at bat and is not motivated by national guilt, philanthropy, or sympathy but, rather, by our national self-interest. But shifting the emphasis toward enabling strategic growth will require the supplier diversity industry to undergo its own transformation, as detailed in later chapters.

TO SUCCEED IS TO SURVIVE, PROSPER, AND GROW TO SCALE

To make their full contribution to the U.S. economy, MBEs must be important members of value chains and large enough to do business with mainstream companies. But for decades, minorities have been allocated token roles *on the periphery* of value chains, which has destined most of them to remain small and insignificant.

It is understandable how this situation came about. Corporations and public-sector agencies came under pressure to do business with minority businesses. The low-risk response was to offer opportunities that involved low barriers to entry and low costs of underperformance. Often, minorities supplied "commodity" items through a bidding process, which resulted in a swarm of desperate MBEs bidding the work down close to their variable costs. This approach allowed corporations to achieve their diversity-spend targets but has caused minorities to remain fringe participants in the mainstream economy.

This situation needs to change.

Minority business owners have the primary responsibility for making progress: they have to earn their place in major value chains. But corporations, public-sector agencies, and support organizations can do more to enable MBE success.

Earning their place in major value chains begins with MBEs overcoming whatever weaknesses are holding them back. Certainly, every business—no matter how large or small, and no matter who owns it—has room for improvement. A well-run business is one that deals with the weaknesses to create a robust platform for future growth.

The starting point in understanding what is needed for MBEs to survive, prosper, and grow to scale is to consider the weaknesses that typically plague small businesses.

THE WEAKNESSES TYPICAL OF MINORITY BUSINESS ENTERPRISES

It is a surprise to many people that access to contracts and access to capital are not the most prominent factors limiting MBE success. Instead, they are the factors that supplier diversity initiatives have found convenient to address. We are learning that providing MBEs with easy access to contracts and capital can actually be counterproductive if the MBE is not set up to deliver on the contracts or to use the capital wisely.

The data we have collected over the years at the Tuck School of Business at Dartmouth[1] pinpoint eight shortcomings that are most likely to hamper MBE success. They are listed in their order of prominence.

1. Lack of strategic clarity.

   This is the greatest problem facing MBEs. Simply put, if MBEs do not know where they are going, they are unlikely to get there. They need a destination and a road map. Entrepreneurs need to be able to answer such basic questions as: What is happening in the market? Where do I fit in the value chain? What is the competitive landscape? What are my sources of competitive advantage? Yet, surprisingly, some state their mission in terms as vague as "I go after every opportunity to make a buck." While this approach seems laudable in that the MBE is focused on generating cash flow, it does not provide the basis for making thoughtful decisions about the business.

   MBEs need to know what business they are in—and what business they are *not* in, so they will not waste time pursuing opportunities at which they cannot succeed. A thoughtful strategy will inform them which customers to pursue, who to hire, whether to buy another business that is for sale, what core competencies to develop, and what the opportunities, as well as the risks, are for significant wealth creation.

2. Reluctance to empower talented, motivated employees.

   Many business owners have trouble "letting go"—allowing their best employees to take the initiative and make things happen. This tendency arises from their need for power and control, which tends to be stronger in managers than in subordinates. But it is often even stronger in entrepreneurs who chose this business role because they do not like other people telling them what to do. It is good for the business owner to have a strong sense of direction, and clear views of how a job should be done, but when taken to extremes, this same conviction can get in the way: the entrepreneur is experienced as a "control freak," not as a strong leader. High-potential employees get frustrated at not being allowed to "run with the ball," and if they do not leave to work elsewhere, they become discontent and withdrawn. Either way, the MBE has lost an opportunity to move the business forward.

3. Poor cash flow management.

Most MBEs do not understand their accounting statements. They offer excuses such as, "That's what I pay my accountant to do," or, "That's just paperwork for taxes." These views are shortsighted, given that a major cause of business failure is not lack of profitability but running out of money to operate the business. The balance sheet tells them what the assets are worth and what claims are placed on those assets, such as debts. The profit-and-loss statement tells them how revenues compare with costs. But neither statement tells them about the *timing* of cash flows.

Timing matters a lot. MBEs usually have to pay their workers and other expenses long before the work is complete and invoiced; then they have to wait for payment from their customers. During this time lag, their bank accounts can run dry. And the faster the business is growing, the greater the problem, because smaller revenues from previous invoices do not finance the larger expenses of upcoming greater business activity. Therefore, it is vital for MBEs to understand what their financial statements are revealing so they can plan and make decisions accordingly.

4. Inadequate control systems.

Controls are systems that allow MBEs to track whether they are making progress toward achieving their various business goals. Control systems compare results with what the MBEs expected. For example, budgets tell them whether more money is being spent than they intended; quality control tells them whether their business is meeting the standards of excellence they set; project management milestones tell them whether they are on schedule to meet the required time deadlines; and performance appraisals tell them whether workers are doing what is expected of them. Some MBEs think that they can get by if they keep track of everything "in their heads," but this becomes increasingly difficult as the business grows. Without control systems, the growing MBE's approach amounts to hoping for the best when in fact the business is "out of control."

5. Ineffective or inefficient processes.

Processes are the set of procedures by which services get delivered—or by which goods get manufactured and put in the customer's hands. Customer satisfaction and profitability can usually be traced back to the adequacy of organizational processes, which is why so many large companies have gone through "business process reengineering" over the past two or three decades.

It is easy to see how ineffective and inefficient processes become established, and then ignored. During the hectic start-up days, MBEs often set up processes with a "get-it-done" attitude. As the business evolves and new challenges pop up, they do not get around to revising the processes to make them effective and lean. Everyone has developed the habit of doing things the old way, the processes become entrenched as standard operating procedures, and the business passes up a primary source of competitive advantage and profitability.

6. Organizational structure gets in the way.

Organizational architecture—the more formal name for the structure of an organization that is often shown as an organization chart—is supposed to facilitate communication, decision making, and accountability. But an outdated or inappropriate structure can easily become a bottleneck that hinders these important organizational functions.

Here is how the structure typically evolves. At start-up, the MBE usually has a handful of people reporting to him or her. If the business is successful and grows, more employees are added, but the MBE who wants to keep tight control adds them to his or her set of "direct reports" and works longer hours to keep things moving. Over time, the growing business will reach a point where there are way too many direct reports to manage, the MBE becomes overwhelmed, and the business becomes paralyzed.

In larger businesses, the MBEs have different problems to contend with. As organizations grow, different functional areas tend to split off into isolated "silos," with workers becoming focused exclusively on their functional area rather than on the organization as a whole. Vertical layers start to emerge too, with managers interacting only with managers at their same level, thereby distancing themselves from the people actually doing the work. The resulting "caste system"—which invariably becomes more entrenched over time—tends to shut down communication among people who need to coordinate with each other, to reduce lower-level workers' sense of inclusion in the enterprise, and to preclude organization-wide commitment to managerial decisions.

7. Being self oriented rather than customer oriented.

Customers buy from a supplier because doing so enables them to meet their needs. One would therefore imagine that all MBEs would orient their businesses toward creating value for their customers. After all, that is how they take business away from competitors, make profits, and ensure that they get repeat business. Yet an amazing number of MBEs, large and small, are unapologetically self oriented. They started the business to enable themselves to do things they like to do, and they want customers to pay them for doing it. But that is not how market mechanisms work.

We have experienced self orientation at the expense of customer orientation when dialing an 800 number to get help and being forced to enter a long series of numbers to get automated responses. That system was not set up for the customer's benefit, it was set up for the company's benefit. The problem is so widespread that we have had to coin the term "user-friendly" to describe what customer oriented means in practice.

MBEs maximize their chance of business success when they start off by learning what creates value for customers, then go into the market with a value proposition that emphasizes how the customer will benefit. They reduce their chances for success when they decide what they want to do and how they want to do it, and then they go into the market trying to persuade customers to give them business.

8. Portfolio too narrow.

It is dangerous to put all of your eggs in one basket. So it is strategically unwise for MBEs to rely too heavily on offering only one major service, having only one major product, or depending on business from one major customer.

The problem arises partly from the life-cycle phenomenon. It has been most obvious in the case of new products, which emerge slowly in the marketplace, sell well when they become widely accepted, become difficult to sell profitably when competitors flood the market, and eventually become passé. Services have similar life cycles, and so do major customers. Cycles can be short or long, but they exist in all domains of business.

As a result, overreliance on a particular service, product, or customer means that the MBE is "betting the farm" that the demand, price point, competitive environment, and supply are static. But business situations are never static. Therefore, MBEs need to have a broad enough portfolio of products/services and customers so they can withstand the ups and downs of business life.

Each of these shortcomings can cause a minority business to plateau or even fail. We need MBEs to grow to scale, but they cannot grow to scale if they cannot survive. So let's consider what MBEs need to do to help ensure their survival.

MBE SURVIVAL REQUIRES A DISCIPLINED APPROACH

To survive, MBEs need to (1) offer a compelling value proposition and (2) be able to deliver on it.

A credible value proposition is the foundation for competitive advantage: it states why the customer should buy from that particular MBE rather than from all of the other possible suppliers in the world.

The MBE can claim to be *better* than the competition; alternatively, the MBE can at least match the competitor's offering and in addition be either *differentiated* in an important way or be the preferred supplier due to features of the *relationship*—such as being the incumbent supplier, the diverse option, or the nicest supplier to deal with.

The value proposition may need to be adjusted when dealing with different customers. For example, it is pointless to stress superior quality or greater flexibility if the buyer is only interested in price; it is equally pointless to stress lower cost if the buyer has a production system that requires a demanding, just-in-time delivery schedule that the MBE is not set up to meet.

There are limits to how much the value proposition can be adjusted to match a particular customer's requirements. For example, an MBE positioned as the low-cost supplier cannot simply cut its prices: it still needs to cover fixed costs and debt obligations, sustain its capacity, and make a profit. In fact, to be the low-cost supplier, every aspect of the MBE business needs to be geared toward driving cost out of the operations. Conversely, if flexibility is paramount, then such cost-saving measures may not be feasible: the highly flexible MBE will not be able to run lean, have a limited service/product line, or purchase raw materials in large batches.

When there is no way to be significantly better than the competition, MBEs can differentiate their offerings in order to appeal to particular market niches. Differentiation enriches the value proposition when the difference is large, important to the customer segment, and fairly unique. A minority-owned printing business that offers embossing of business cards will have only a small advantage over printers that do not. An MBE with a top security clearance will have an advantage over other suppliers to some customers, but not to others. An MBE that offers recycled paper for copying machines is hardly unique, but one that is nearby and also repairs office machines may be the only such supplier.

While differentiation can be a strategic advantage when the difference is important to particular customers, it can be a strategic weakness if it narrows the set of customers enough to create overdependency. *Long-term survival is put at risk when any customer accounts for more of the revenue stream than the MBE can afford to lose.* No supplier-customer arrangement is perpetual: customers revise strategy, change policies, replace purchasing agents, and go bankrupt. Hoping that none of these developments occurs is a high-stakes gamble. It is hard for any business to take in stride the loss of a major revenue stream, therefore, a wise rule of thumb is for the MBE never to have more than 30 percent of the total business volume coming from one customer.

If the risk of narrowing the customer base is manageable, then differentiation can increase the appeal of the value proposition, but the MBE needs to emphasize that the customer is not making a significant sacrifice to take advantage of the difference. The appeal needs to be of the form, "We offer the same essential value you get from competitors, *and more*. Here's what is special about buying from us . . ." Some products and services—such as janitorial supplies or IT staffing—are very hard to differentiate; in such cases, MBEs will have to be better on some dimension, such as lower price or greater responsiveness. Being a diverse business can significantly differentiate the business in some procurement situations, but if there are no other benefits, then diverse status is unlikely to create a sustainable competitive advantage for the MBE.

Aspects of the relationship can motivate purchasing behavior even when the offering is neither better nor differentiated. It should be no surprise that, all things being equal, purchasing agents will prefer to have a pleasant experience when allocating business. But the strongest relationship dimension of the purchasing process is not liking but incumbency. Repeat business is easier to get because purchasing agents have a bias toward awarding contracts to suppliers who have done an adequate job in the past: the risk of nonperformance is low compared to a supplier they have never dealt with before.

Note that relationship strength is more often an inhibitor than a facilitator of MBE success. For example, if white male purchasing agents have been giving business to white male suppliers, then minorities and women will be at a disadvantage simply because of comfort and familiarity. That is why organizations need supplier diversity professionals to intervene in habitual decision making and to persuade purchasing agents to give MBEs an opportunity to show that they can perform.

MBES MUST DELIVER ON THE VALUE PROPOSITION

A compelling value proposition creates the potential for the MBE to survive in a competitive, dynamic marketplace, but the MBE must deliver on it. This requires a holistic, disciplined approach to running the enterprise;

otherwise, the business is likely to experience many of the weaknesses listed in the beginning of this chapter.

A disciplined approach consists of assessing what areas need improvement, fixing the problems, and then making sure all of the managerial components of the business are in alignment. The essential managerial components are shown in Figure 2.1.

The MBE's survival depends on how well it creates value for *customers*. That is why customers are placed at the very top of the figure. The MBE's *strategy* is inherently customer focused: it dictates whether competitive advantage will come from being better than competitors, being different, or being the preferred supplier due to relationship strength.

In practice, what actually creates value for customers is a set of *processes*. Traditionally, scholars have focused on the products and services that

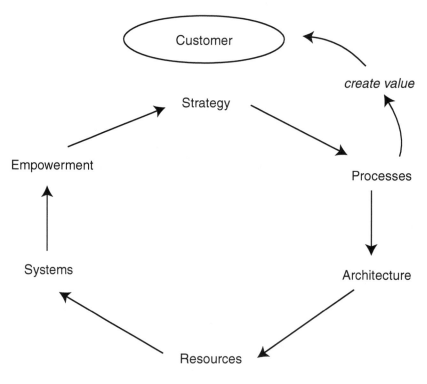

FIGURE 2.1
Strategic Alignment of the Minority Business Enterprise

organizations provide when evaluating market appeal. But it is more useful to focus on processes. Suppose, for example, that you need a hotel room for business travel. Objectively, you are renting a bed. But you do not experience the bed most of the time that you are using it because you are asleep. What creates value is efficient processes. You want to go to your room as soon as possible: you do not want to stand in line waiting to register. The same is true at checkout time. And you want room-service meals to arrive at the time you are hungry and asked for them, not within a half-hour "window" that maximizes the hotel's convenience. The processes create the value.

Processes are now recognized as being so important that most organizations have gone through business process reengineering. This involves systematically analyzing key business processes and then figuring out how to improve them. Done properly, a reengineering program aligns processes with strategy. *An MBE cannot achieve its strategic goals unless the right processes are in place.* And MBEs gain competitive advantage when their processes create superior value for their customers than their competitors create.

Smaller companies seldom can afford to pay reengineering experts to come in and redesign their processes, but 80 percent of the improvement can be achieved by the MBE simply charting key processes and figuring out how the current way of doing things can be improved. Typical questions to pose when reviewing each process—or each step of a complex process—include: Is this adding value to the customer (and, if not, can this step be eliminated)? Is there a simpler way of achieving this end result? Are our key customers happy with the way we do things?

Next, the MBE needs to have the right organizational *architecture in* place. Architecture is the management structure that enables reporting and decision making. It is shown in an organization chart. Minority business owners typically face three challenges when coming up with the right architecture for their business. As entrepreneurs, they tend to retain control when they ought to be delegating; when they grow, they do not adjust the structure to reflect the larger scale; and they design a structure without considering the processes the structure is supposed to implement.

To clarify the third point, processes work well when there is cooperation between functional areas. If the structure keeps people in isolated silos, then processes break down and the business loses efficiency and competitive advantage. For example, salespeople need to sell what is most profitable, but they cannot do this if they never talk to the accounting people. They cannot ensure delivery as promised if they do not talk to the warehouse people, who in turn cannot maintain an adequate inventory if they never talk to the manufacturing people. While control-freaks inhibit the lateral integration of growing enterprises, silos strangle process coordination in large enterprises. Getting the architecture right is very important to MBE success.

When processes and architecture are in place to carry out the strategy, the manager's attention can turn to securing the right *resources*: people, technology, and capital. The MBE needs enough people with the appropriate skills to do the organization's tasks, working effectively in groups. (Think about it: it is almost always groups, rather than individuals, that carry out processes.) Acquiring the right technology is a managerial decision: if technology enthusiasts specify the technology, such as IT, then what gets acquired is often too sophisticated for the average user in the company. The other vital resource is capital. Minority business owners need to understand how it is managed, because what often gets construed as an external problem of difficult access to capital turns out to be an internal problem of cash flow management.

With the right resources available, *systems* need to be in place to ensure that strategy is being implemented on time, efficiently, and according to plan. The most important systems are measurement of key business outcomes, controls that correct performance that is below expectations, and clear communication about what employees ought to be doing and why.

It is especially important for MBEs to make sure that systems are tailored to processes. For example, if strategy implementation requires a collaborative process between employees, but systems measure and reward each employee's *individual* performance, then the misalignment of systems and processes will undermine cooperation, which makes it more difficult to create customer value.

Finally, business owners need to make the decisions that they are in the best position to make. But they also need to be able to delegate decisions to their workers—to *empower* them to take the initiative—when employees are in a better position to make these decisions. In entre-preneurial organizations, decisions tend to be made by the owner, who might really believe she or he is the only one qualified to make such calls. But the people who are actually doing the work are often—perhaps usually—in the best position to know what improvements need to be made. So if workers are not allowed to make decisions, then the only improve-ments that will be made are those that somehow come to the attention of the owner. Thus *empowerment is a source of competitive advantage because it is the key to improving customer satisfaction, innovation, and continuous improvement.*

A disciplined approach to organizational improvement involves work-ing sequentially through the model. The circle of arrows in Figure 2.1 shows how the managerial elements need to be integrated. The MBE's strategy will determine what processes are necessary to create value for customers. The processes will drive architectural form: they will create the need for particular forms of coordination. The resulting organization will have to be properly staffed and supplied with the other resources it needs. Then systems will have to be put into place to ensure that the strat-egy is being implemented efficiently. And key employees will have to be empowered to achieve the continuous improvement needed to stay ahead of competitors—which is the ultimate objective of a business strategy.

The arrows depict a cycle because integration is not something a busi-ness owner does once and for all, as in the case of designing a machine. Each element in the cycle needs to be constantly monitored and adjusted because businesses operate in a constantly changing environment. The competitive landscape shifts, new processes are introduced, architecture evolves as better suppliers replace mediocre suppliers, resources become scarce or abundant, new systems are made possible due to technological evolution (bar codes and embedded smart chips might be good examples of innovations that transform systems), and empowered workers make adaptive changes. Business owners may need to compensate for the change in any element by appropriate changes in other elements, so as to restore alignment.

Perpetually striving for excellence and alignment is vital for MBE survival because it is a source of competitive advantage. Doing well is not enough in today's global marketplace: you always need to do better. Competitors monitor a company that is doing well (they call it "benchmarking"), and they try to copy whatever is creating competitive advantage. If you are constantly optimizing and realigning each factor, then by the time competitors have caught up with what your company used to be doing you will have become even better. So then they have to reach for the higher standard you have set. If you do a good enough job of staying ahead of the competition, then they will get discouraged and shift their efforts to another market niche. Thus excellence and continuous improvement are great "barriers to entry" into any company's domain, and perhaps the major source of competitive advantage these days.

PROSPERING DEPENDS ON INDUSTRY STAGE AND VALUE-CHAIN POSITION

The minority-owned firm's potential to generate wealth is determined by the industry in which it is operating and the MBE's place in the value chain. Some industries have limited profit potential no matter where the MBE is in the value chain; other industries have plenty of profit potential, but MBEs need to have the right value-chain role to capture the generous revenue streams.

Many factors affect the profit potential in particular industries, but it is important to realize that the situation is dynamic, not static. What appears lucrative today may be lean tomorrow, and vice versa. Thus MBEs must forecast future developments as well as assess current opportunities. Let's consider two industries—health care and transportation—to understand how opportunities can vary even within an industry.

Health care is generally a promising industry, but MBEs are not going to find all parts of the industry equally accessible. The nursing home industry is likely to grow. The baby boom generation is approaching retirement, and life expectancy has increased. Therefore, the number of people seeking long-term care is certain to increase as time goes on. This tends to be a local industry that is not vulnerable to offshoring: people are unlikely to ship their aging relatives off to China to take advantage of low labor rates, even though the idea might have some appeal from time to time. And it is relatively easy to get into the nursing home business.

The vaccine industry is another health care industry that is likely to grow, but the opportunities for MBEs are not as accessible. The vaccine business will continue to be lucrative because health care costs will always need to be contained, and disease prevention is more efficient than managing and curing illness. But the industry is not easy for MBEs to enter due to regulatory controls, the need for special qualifications, and high insurance premiums. And, unlike nursing homes, there is no advantage to being local: vaccines can be developed and manufactured anywhere in the world, and shipping costs are low.

Transportation is a less promising industry overall. The auto industry continues to offer large-volume outsourcing opportunities, and it has a long history of proactively involving diverse suppliers. But the profit potential will remain low due to the excess in global manufacturing capacity resulting in severe competition among manufacturers, who in turn push their suppliers for price concessions. The industry will rebound from recession, and the strongest suppliers will survive. In contrast, the corporate jet industry, once lucrative, is in a long-term, steep decline. Its demise is due to rising public outrage over excessive executive "benefits," shareholder resistance to having profits diverted to unjustifiable expenses, and—increasingly important—the unacceptable environmental impact of flying a jet plane with one or a small number of passengers when transportation options are available that have much lower carbon emissions.

Other sectors within transportation are growing, are more lucrative, and are more accessible. Airports, roads, and bridges are always being rebuilt and maintained. The demand for mass transit is increasing. And alternatives to travel—such as videoconferencing—present opportunities with low barriers to entry.

Thus the MBE needs to go beyond industry choice to examine specific opportunities within industries. But even a good opportunity will not be a good opportunity forever, because the business situation is dynamic, not static.

All business initiatives have life cycles. These are easy to recognize in the case of new products, such as iPhones, or services, such as IT staffing. They start out with limited customer interest, grow in volume and profitability, mature and become saturated with competitors, and eventually decline.

Getting involved at the very outset of a life cycle may not be the best strategy for the MBE. New industries demand cash outlays up front, with revenues trickling in until the industry gets established: this can create cash flow demands that few MBEs can comfortably accommodate. The growth period is usually the most profitable, particularly when supply cannot keep up with demand. The diminished prosperity problem emerges in the mature phase, when lots of competitors enter the market and drive down profit margins. In the decline phase, demand collapses faster than suppliers can exit the industry, leaving them struggling for whatever business remains, or narrowing their focus to serve the remaining niches (there used to be a travel agent in every shopping center . . .).

In sum, the ability of the MBE to prosper may depend largely on the choice of industry. If the industry is in decline, or if the lucrative parts of it are difficult to access, then a wise MBE will assess whether the core competency of the business is transferable. As examples, a minority business owner that knows how to run a motel can learn how to run a nursing home. An MBE that is manufacturing prototype parts for the auto industry can probably supply replacement parts for planes and military vehicles no longer being manufactured but still in service. And a minority-owned IT firm with a security clearance ought to be able to digitize health care records.

VALUE-CHAIN ROLE DETERMINES MBE PROSPERITY

After making a wise choice about which industry to serve, the MBE must pursue a value-chain role that offers the opportunity for profitable growth.

Figure 2.2 shows a simplified, generic manufacturing chain. Let's suppose the manufactured product is an automobile. Raw materials such as steel, rubber, and plastic resin are not very valuable in their unrefined state, but value is added when these are stamped or molded into components such as gas tanks, tires, and steering wheels. When the components are assembled to become a drivable car, additional value has been created. When the car is on-site at a local dealership, even more value has been added because the car has been transported nearby and made avail-

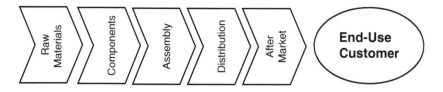

FIGURE 2.2
A Simple Manufacturing Value Chain—Automobiles

able for a test drive. Further value is added by businesses that perform services such as financing, insurance, maintenance, and refueling.

In the automotive example, a considerable amount of value has been added by the time iron ore has been transformed into something that provides income for an insurance agent. Members of the value chain are rewarded for increasing the product's value, but the rewards are not equally distributed: some value contributors are rewarded handsomely, while others are rewarded meagerly. For example, component suppliers make little money from their efforts; finance companies make a lot by comparison. This is a very important point for minority business owners to keep in mind. *The ability to generate wealth depends on where the MBE is located in the value chain.*

Service value chains tend to be more complex, but they are analyzed the same way. Figure 2.3 shows a simplified service value chain involving U.S. tax-return preparation. Many taxpayers find the IRS tax codes difficult to apply optimally to their own situation. As a result, value is added when experts interpret the latest tax regulations and create decision trees. But all of this knowledge resides inside the head of the tax expert. So value is added when the decision trees are written into lines of code that become software. For taxpayers who have complex tax situations or are uncomfortable using the software, specialists add value by preparing their returns. Further value is added when the specialist submits the return to the IRS. Value has been added at each link in the value chain, but the profitability of each value-added contribution is different.

Many value chains involve both products and services, and these are analyzed the same way. Figure 2.4 shows a simplified service/manufacturing value chain that results in a child being vaccinated. Value is added

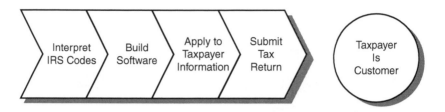

FIGURE 2.3
A Simple Service Value Chain—Tax Preparation

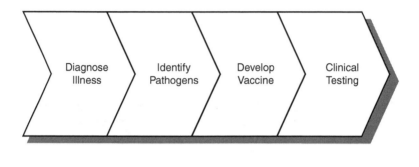

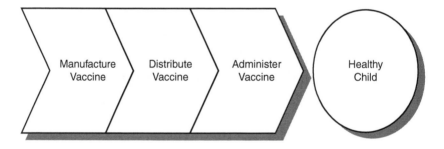

FIGURE 2.4
A Simple Service/Manufacturing Value Chain—Vaccination

when symptoms of sickness are transformed into a diagnosis. Further value is created when the germs that cause the sickness have been isolated and identified, then when a vaccine is developed to create antibodies in children's immune systems, and next when the vaccine is tested in clinical trials to ensure it is effective and not harmful. From here we move to the manufacturing domain, with further value being created when the manufactured vaccine is distributed to clinics, hospitals, and doctors' offices. The final opportunity for value creation is in the administration of the dose. As is typical, contributors to this value chain are not equally rewarded.

The three different examples of value chains were presented because it is vital for MBEs—and the organizations that foster their economic success—to understand the value chains in which MBEs are embedded. Simply put, *MBEs are unlikely to prosper unless they understand their value chain, how they fit into it, and where the opportunities for growth and profitability are.*

MBEs need to be proactive in seeking out a favorable value-chain role because they are likely to be assigned a peripheral role—or, at best, a low-revenue position—if they wait for someone to issue a request for quote (RFQ). Corporations tend to perform high-profit activities in-house; they outsource activities from which there is little money to be made. And if they are under pressure to achieve diversity-spend targets, then the low-risk approach is to buy goods and services that make no difference to the corporation's value-adding activities—for example, by purchasing promotional products, landscaping, or office supplies.

As a result, MBEs that approach the market passively are unlikely to become integrated into major supply chains. Prosperity will be elusive because the revenue stream will come in spurts, contract by contract, and margins will be depressed by hungry suppliers bidding down prices. The MBE can settle for this peripheral business or strive to achieve a strategic role in the value chain—a role where the MBE's contribution makes a difference to the customer's competitive advantage.

The largest impact will come from the minority business owner understanding the value chain in which he or she is currently operating and learning where the most money is to be made. Business owners tend to know a lot about their own industries, but they rarely figure out that they can make a lot more money by moving downstream or upstream in their own value chain—that is, by taking over their supplier's position or their customer's.

An MBE whose business is installing swimming pools may make more money selling them or cleaning and maintaining them. An MBE selling steel storage buildings may make more money as the general contractor or as the property owner who leases out the building spaces. The MBE providing temporary staffing might make more money doing permanent placement (or, in a recession, outplacement), or providing a turnkey "back-office" service to businesses. In each case, the MBE will analyze the value-chain, figure out where the high-profit opportunity is, and transform the business to take over that role.

MBES HAVE THREE OPTIONS FOR GROWING TO SCALE

It is common to speak of minority-owned firms surviving, prospering, and growing to scale, in that order. The MBE has to survive to stay in the game and then prosper to reinvest in the business and finance the expansion.

But in many cases, scale is so important that it is required for survival in the industry. For example, in the auto industry, the manufacturers are not economically viable unless they build vehicles by the thousands; therefore, small-scale suppliers simply cannot provide the volume efficiencies the auto companies need. In that industry, the MBE does not create a small business and grow it to scale; the supplier operation needs to be started up as a large-scale business.

MBE scale may also be necessary to survive and prosper in an era of supply-base consolidation. Today, major U.S.-based corporations have to withstand global competition; they cannot absorb the inefficiencies of dealing with a large number of small suppliers; they need to deal with a small number of large suppliers. So MBEs have to be large in order to be eligible for supply contracts.

The three basic options for increasing scale are organic growth, acquisition, and strategic alliance. Each option has advantages and disadvantages, and managing the resulting larger enterprises poses its own set of challenges: medium-size businesses are qualitatively different from small ones, and large businesses are different yet again. Not every minority business owner aspires to make the transformation, and of those that do, few have the knowledge and experience to run a larger-scale business.

ORGANIC GROWTH IS A SLOW, NONLINEAR PROGRESSION

Most entrepreneurial businesses start out as a small face-to-face operation. If they are successful, they add sales volume, hire more employees, get a bigger credit line, and move into larger facilities. This process results in growth but does not put them on a pathway to becoming a large corporation. Several transformations are necessary along the way.

When entrepreneurs outgrow the face-to-face organization that took them through the start-up phase, they have to delegate the day-to-day management of the company to professional managers. The owner's job is to ensure the organization's ability to deliver on its value proposition. She or he needs to assess what areas need improvement, fix the problems, and then make sure all of the managerial components of the business are in alignment, as we saw in Figure 2.1.

When the organization becomes large, the owner's role is another step removed from the business, focusing on strategy rather than on tactics, setting targets and keeping track of progress through reports, and managing relationships with customers, suppliers, bankers, regulators, and the community.

Organic growth places a burden on cash flow. At the outset of a growth spurt, more employees need to be hired, larger buildings need to be built or rented, and more equipment needs to be purchased. These expenses must be covered right away. But it takes time for the increased revenue to come in from the subsequent higher sales volume. The profit-and-loss statement paints a rosy picture, with accounts receivable swollen, fixed costs being amortized over time, and depreciation reducing the tax obligations. But cash has been drained from the business, to be replenished at some point in the future—if the MBE can finance the cash shortfall.

GROWTH BY ACQUISITION REQUIRES DUE DILIGENCE

Acquisition is a fast way to achieve scale. The minority business owner simply buys the additional capacity.

Acquisitions need to be strategic rather than opportunistic: MBEs cannot afford to make the "yard sale error," whereby people sell things they do not need to other people who do not need them either but cannot pass up such a bargain! A strategically wise reason for buying another business is that it increases capacity to create value for customers and competitive advantage. If the acquisition accomplishes neither, then the money the MBE spends is a donation, not an investment.

If the acquisition makes strategic sense, then three key questions need to be addressed:

- Why is the business for sale? MBEs should *avoid* buying businesses that are about to lose their major customers or essential employees, businesses that have lawsuits or environmental liabilities pending, businesses that have insurmountable debts, or businesses that face the same problems that threaten the MBE's long-term viability. MBEs should *consider* buying businesses that could be highly profitable if run well, businesses that create synergies whereby the existing and acquired enterprises are better off working jointly than each working independently, or businesses that are being sold because the owner's heirs do not want to take over the business.

- How will the MBE finance the acquisition? The MBE will have to finance not only the purchase price but also the acquired company's working capital. Access to capital tends to be difficult for minorities and women in the best of times, and tight credit markets do not help at all. The debt capacity of the combined companies will have to be carefully evaluated before proceeding very far down the path toward acquisition.

- Who will manage the larger enterprise? Most minority business owners have their hands full managing the business they already have. An acquired business needs their attention and their time, especially during the ownership transition. In general, the smaller the enterprise, the more time the owner spends working *in* the business. He or she may be reluctant to give up control, but delegating current responsibilities is usually essential for taking on new ones.

It is important for minorities seeking to expand their business volume to know that most acquisitions fail—that is, they leave the purchaser worse off than before. This is not a reason to eliminate acquisition as a growth option, but it is a reason to exercise due diligence. The failures can almost always be traced to bad decision making at the outset or poor management of the transition, and only rarely to a market situation collapsing.

STRATEGIC ALLIANCE IS AN ALTERNATIVE
TO ACQUISITION

A strategic alliance is an enduring relationship between two companies that is designed to achieve mutual gain.[2] Let's examine the terms we just used to describe it. An *alliance* is different from a transaction in that allied companies have made a commitment to do business together beyond the immediate deal—that is what makes the relationship *enduring*. An alliance is *strategic* if it has a significant impact on competitive advantage, that is, if it allows an MBE to get business that might otherwise go to a competitor. *Mutual gain* is achieved when each company, working together, achieves results that are better than each could achieve working alone.

There are two major motives for MBEs to form strategic alliances: the MBEs are too small to satisfy contract requirements working alone, or their core competencies and capacity only allow them to do part of a job.

As an example of the motivation to achieve functional scale, think of an MBE-owned trucking company that has a good record of providing statewide transportation services but has the opportunity to make a lot more money if it can offer nationwide service. The MBE may not have the resources to achieve the required geographic scale in time to take advantage of the current contract opportunity but can achieve the effects of national scale by partnering with a large trucking company that can handle the out-of-state transportation.

An example of motivation to ally due to insufficient core competency or capacity would be if the same small MBE-owned trucking company encountered an attractive multiyear within-state contract opportunity where the client needed logistic support and extensive warehouse storage as well as transportation. In the latter case, the MBE can satisfy its client's needs by partnering with a logistics company to supplement core competencies and with a warehousing company to create capacity.

Mutual gain is achieved in both of these scenarios because the MBE and the partnered businesses gain a revenue stream they would not obtain if working alone.

MBEs can choose from the array of alternative business relationships shown in Figure 2.5. The appropriate choice would take into account the

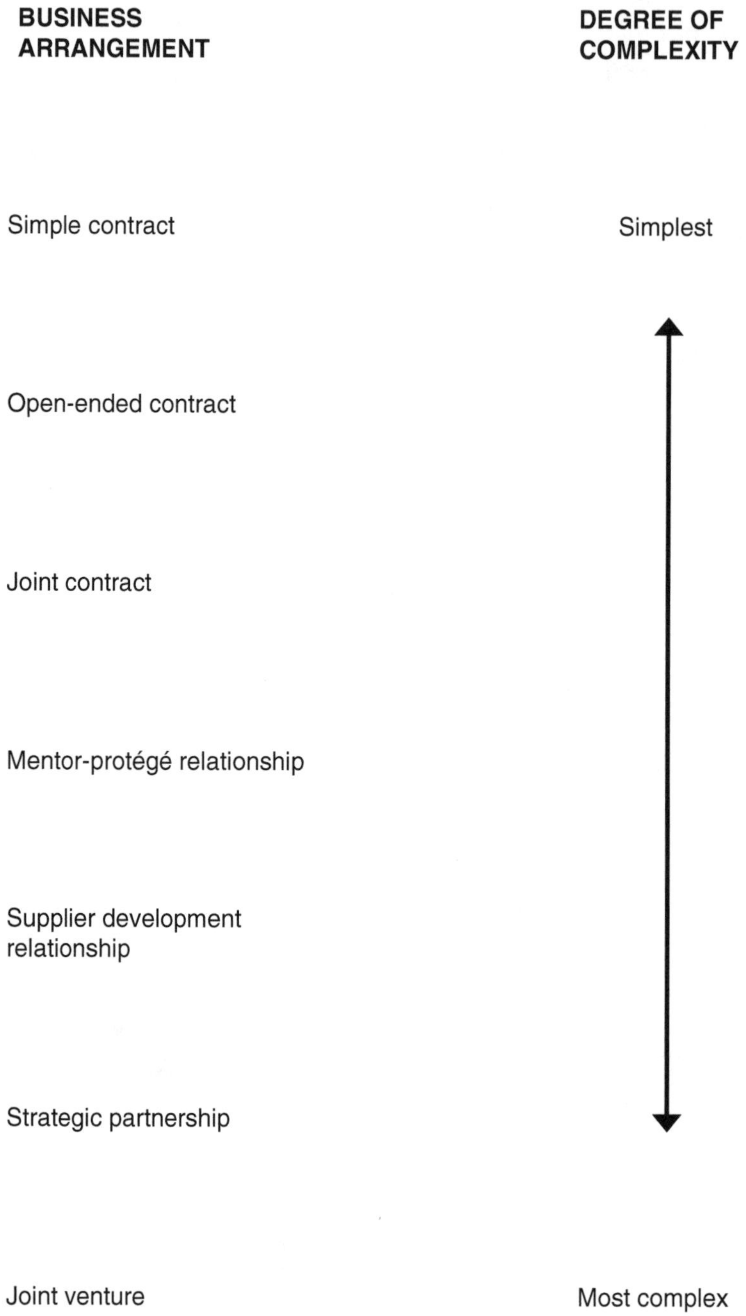

BUSINESS ARRANGEMENT	DEGREE OF COMPLEXITY
Simple contract	Simplest
Open-ended contract	↑
Joint contract	
Mentor-protégé relationship	
Supplier development relationship	
Strategic partnership	↓
Joint venture	Most complex

FIGURE 2.5
Options for MBE Business Relationships

strategic objective, the risks, and the degree of control sought. The options are listed from the simplest arrangement to the most complex.

Simple contract: This basic transaction occurs when a business offer is accepted and something of value is exchanged. A contract is specific about what is expected of each party. It does not obligate the businesses to any future deals. Simple contracts can be used to replace trust in a vendor-buyer relationship, to impose penalties for disappointing performance, or sometimes to communicate unambiguously what has been agreed to. When companies issue an RFQ, for example, it is usually for a specific supply arrangement. By responding, the MBE makes a commitment to comply with the terms of the RFQ and can subsequently be sued for noncompliance.

Open-ended contract: This arrangement is specific about the terms on which the companies will do business, but perhaps not specific about how much business will be done or when. It can represent more or less of a commitment to do business; the range of possibilities includes licensing or franchise agreements, or contracts to produce goods under a private label. A *sole-source* open-ended contract commits the buyer to deal only with the supplier. An *exclusive* open-ended contract guarantees that other customers will not receive goods and services from this supplier. Whatever the specifics, there may be little to the relationship beyond what is required in the contract.[3]

Joint contract: A company can contract with two or more other entities to supply services or goods. The suppliers' relationship is usually one we would characterize as a strategic alliance. It could be that the two suppliers are working together very closely and the contract has the primary purpose of communicating what the client expects of them. But it could also be essentially a separate contract with each of them, with the client managing the vendor-supplier relationship and thereby insulating its business from possible relationship problems between the two suppliers.

Mentor-protégé relationship: People acquire wisdom with age, usually as a result of trial and error. A personal mentor can accelerate the learning process, be a sounding board for ideas, and give the protégé access to the mentor's network. Minority business enterprises likewise typically have limited know-how in their early years, a phenomenon known to organizational scholars as "the liability of newness."[4] Established companies can be more or less helpful in getting fledgling enterprises through the challenges of their early years. At the less-helpful extreme, large corporations assign a middle manager to "talk to the MBE" so that the company can check off a box required for contract compliance. At the most-helpful extreme, the MBE is coached to succeed by experienced people who want to "give back" and who can provide meaningful guidance because they understand the MBE's business.

Supplier development relationship: The nature of competition has changed. Only a few decades ago, the primary competition was between large, vertically integrated companies vying for share of stable domestic markets; today, competition is between rival value chains struggling for share of rapidly evolving global markets. With the trend away from vertical integration and toward outsourcing, competitive advantage (and disadvantage) can arise from various points in the value chain, so the strength of the value chain really matters. It is therefore important to global businesses that minority suppliers develop into strong value-chain partners. An investment in the development of an MBE is an investment in the corporation's own competitive advantage.

Strategic partnership: Here the two or more suppliers have coordinated their strategies so that they have become either dependent on each other or have made a binding commitment to seek business together. The partnering relationship can be formalized in a legal arrangement or based on the integrity of a promise.

Joint venture: A joint venture, as the term is used here, is a legally independent business entity that is owned by the strategic allies. It operates entrepreneurially, drawing on resources as needed from the parent organizations. It is distinct from a strategic partnership in that *a new organization is created* for the purpose of achieving competitive advantage that neither parent organization could accomplish alone. Minority entrepreneurs can create joint ventures, but for many contract domains, they need to know how the ownership arrangement affects their minority status.

The point of explaining the various options for business relationships is to clear up misunderstandings of what the terminology means and to identify the implications for how the business will be run as some sort of a collaborative—and perhaps even joint—entity. Strategic alliances are business relationships formed for a purpose, and that purpose, ultimately, is to create value for customers and gain competitive advantage.

ENABLING MBE GROWTH IS IMPORTANT AND WORTHWHILE

It is in the interest of the nation to foster the growth to scale of minority-owned businesses. MBEs need to take their place in value chains and create the level of economic impact the national economy increasingly depends on. Minority businesses are the most promising source of job creation for minorities.[5] The small ones do not hire any outside employees; the larger businesses hire hundreds, create wealth that can be re-spent in the local economy, provide career paths, and create positive role models.

It is in the interest of major corporations to foster growth to scale of the future supply chain, which, due to changing demographics, will necessarily be diverse. In addition to investing in the vitality and competitive advantage of the value chain, corporations need to think about the advantages of a positive corporate reputation among minorities and women. These populations make up the workforce and the consumer base of the future. Corporations that are viewed as a good place to work—and as a good corporate citizen to buy from—will have a competitive advantage over corporations that are insensitive to the rapidly changing composition of their consumer and labor markets. Public policy decisions that foster positive relationships with minority and women voters will realize loyalty benefits into the future. Thus there is a clear "business case" to be made for enabling the success of diverse businesses.

We need to enable MBEs to become large-scale enterprises—by eliminating the barriers as well as guiding the progress. The barriers in public policy emanate from the notion that we should be helping minorities rise above poverty, but we should not be helping them become rich and influential. MBEs get kicked out of the 8(a) program, for example, if they accumulate enough personal assets to own a house in a middle-class community and send their kids to college. It is in the public interest to keep such people on the growth trajectory, yet well-intentioned public policy has the unintended consequence of penalizing success.

Government agencies are the instruments of public policy, and can—and, as we will see in Chapter 3, should—make a real difference in diverse inclusion. They can provide access to contracts and capital and require their tiers of suppliers to buy from and help develop diverse businesses. Corporate supplier diversity programs are also an obvious means of enabling growth, and these will be discussed at length in Chapter 4.

Both public-sector and private-sector procurement functions must deal with the cycle of exclusion. There are only a limited number of diverse suppliers to buy from due to historical discrimination; if they continue to buy from current majority suppliers that are already of scale, then diverse businesses will continue to suffer the consequences of historical discrimination. It is a national imperative, as well as a business necessity, to break this cycle, and it represents an investment in the future value chain.

As we will see in Chapter 6, future-oriented procurement strategy involves not just buying from today's best suppliers but developing tomorrow's highest-potential suppliers. Developing them includes coaching them, giving them access to one's own training programs and consultants, offering accounts-payable terms that ease their cash-flow burdens, and investing in the ones that can benefit from "roll-ups" (essentially, buying up small competitors) and standing up businesses that qualified minorities can run and own.

IN SUM . . .

In sum, progress toward economic inclusion of minorities calls for the creation of MBEs that are of sufficient scale to be value-creating members of major value chains. These businesses are the most-likely source of minority job creation, the foundation of local economies, and the major contributors to tomorrow's value chains. Much of the responsibility for surviving, prospering, and becoming positioned for growth rests with minority business owners. But it is in the national interest—and the self-interest of major corporations—to do all they can to help them achieve success.

The ensuing chapters will discuss how public policy can be more helpful, how corporate supplier diversity programs need to evolve, what support organizations can do to achieve greater impact, and the elements of a new paradigm for economic inclusion of minorities.

3 GOVERNMENT MUST REFOCUS
ON INCLUSION

EXECUTIVE SUMMARY

Government has a vital role to play in fostering the development of the nation's commercial activities. This is especially true of the federal government, which must serve the national interest whether or not state and local governments are doing their parts.

The form of the assistance needs to be tailored to business size: small start-up businesses have vastly different challenges than do medium-size businesses, which are different yet again from those challenges facing large businesses. Beyond differences resulting from scale, there are unique business situations and special needs that need to be addressed. Minorities, Native Americans, women, veterans, and businesses operating in inner cities and poor rural areas all have special needs, and it is in the public interest to foster the economic self-sufficiency and success of all. The challenge is to distinguish the role of each government agency and ensure that they work together—and collaborate with corporations and support organizations—to achieve optimum impact and the most efficient use of tax dollars.

Governmental programs are essential because we cannot risk allowing market dynamics to determine the fate of the entrepreneurial economy: there is too much at stake. Small business is the source of wealth and job creation, the petri dish for innovation, and the staging ground for growth and renewal of Corporate America. As minority-owned businesses grow as a percentage of the entrepreneurial sector, their success will determine the vitality of the U.S. economy and our national competitive advantage in the global economy. Their success also plays a key role in implementing the nation's community development and urban strategies: minority businesses are a key source of jobs for minorities, and they are needed to create vibrant local economies, jobs, economic stimulus, career paths, and positive role models for young people in distressed inner cities.

Minority businesses need special attention because they have experienced historical exclusion from important sectors of the economy. Yet despite their ever-increasing importance, efforts of government agencies to ensure their survival, prosperity, and growth to scale have been underfunded and fragmented. Accountability for fostering the success of particular groups is diffuse, mandates are not enforced, and when we have paid attention to the issues at all we have focused on effort rather than impact. A different approach is urgently needed: as the minority population grows inexorably toward becoming the majority before mid-century, the problem of economic underparticipation is growing faster than the solutions we are applying to facilitate their economic inclusion.

The greatest impact will come from integration of the various programs. For this purpose, the White House needs to appoint a *Special Assistant to the President for Diverse Business* to provide horizontal coordination and ensure that the special needs of population subgroups are met, and to ensure role alignment and collaboration.

The U.S. Small Business Administration (SBA) should continue to focus on start-up and fledgling businesses and to administer targeted interventions such as the HUB Zone and 8(a) programs. The SBA has a large decentralized system of client-facing service providers, who should be trained to function effectively as consultants and financial advisors. The SBA needs to avoid overreliance on technology-based services such as distance learning, because many of the neediest business owners are not computer literate or have poor access to broadband; and, the most important business skills to develop—those involving strategic and financial judgment—are not effectively developed by distance learning.

The U.S. Department of Commerce, which houses the Minority Business Development Agency (MBDA), would be mandated to implement a National Industrial Strategy by fostering the establishment, survival, and development of industry clusters and infrastructure needed to maintain America's place in the global economy. The minority-owned businesses that can be grown to scale and contribute to the strategy should be supported by a refocused MBDA with its role revised to supplement rather than replicate what the SBA does. MBDA should be structured like a major consulting firm and its processes reengineered to reflect its new strategic focus.

The U.S. Department of the Interior administers treaty-based intergovernmental relationships with American Indian sovereign nations. It needs to continue its role in helping tribes achieve economic self-sufficiency by fostering the success of tribally owned businesses. But it also needs to nurture entrepreneurial activity in Native communities in order to sustain local economies by encouraging the recirculation of revenues. The Interior Department needs to work collaboratively with the SBA and MBDA, and they collectively need to work in concert with other agencies involved in Indian country.

Because the needed realignment of governmental agencies is broad in scope, it cannot be accomplished without White House involvement. Most of this nation's major inclusion initiatives—including economic policy, set-asides, affirmative action, school desegregation, welfare, and environmental policy—were put into place during the Nixon administration, which empowered Robert J. Brown to "make it happen" by coordinating and refocusing divergent governmental programs. That same mandate and leadership is needed today.

The objective would be to align Cabinet-level directives, eliminate duplication, focus on achieving real impact, resolve territorial disputes that arise between agencies, ensure compliance with existing governmental mandates, and hold leaders accountable for interagency collaboration. The office would also serve in a liaison role with the various interest groups and support organizations that serve the diverse business domain.

GOVERNMENT MUST REFOCUS ON INCLUSION

In the civil rights era of the 1960s and 1970s, inclusion of minorities and women was construed as a social issue. Attention was focused on discrimination in the sociopolitical realm—such as who could vote, who could sit at lunch counters or in the front of the bus, and who could attend particular schools. Those dehumanizing practices are no longer institutionalized, but *discrimination remains in effect, primarily in the economic domain*: minorities and women are not participating in the U.S. economy at a level commensurate with their representation in the general population.

The underparticipation of minorities and women should concern us not just because it is unfair—which it certainly is—but, rather, because it is contrary to the national interest. We need everyone's economic contribution. Not only have we been in a difficult period of economic recovery, we are struggling to retain our premier position in the global economy. That is why it is the responsibility of government to give every potential contributor a fair chance to succeed.

Economic interventions cannot hope to be cost-effective, or effective at all, if they are approached in a piecemeal fashion—that is, if they are designed to deal expeditiously with one symptom after the next. Somebody needs to be looking at the total picture of economic inclusion of our increasingly diverse business system so that we address root causes, not just symptoms, and that somebody almost certainly needs to be located in the White House.

We need a *Special Assistant to the President for Diverse Business* to provide "horizontal" coordination of the programs of the various agencies, shape the direction of congressional committees that determine priorities and authorize funding, enforce the mandates that are currently being ignored without consequences, and align state and local government programs with nongovernmental efforts to achieve the system-level goals.

We know from history that appointing a strong leader to implement an explicit presidential mandate can be highly effective in producing results. Richard Nixon put into place school desegregation, affirmative action, minority set-asides, welfare reform, economic policy, and environmental policy in the adverse political and social environment of the period 1968–1974. Nixon's appointee, Robert J. Brown, was told to "make it happen" and gained Cabinet-level compliance due to having strong White House backing. If so much progress could be made during the Nixon era, just imagine what could have been accomplished during the Carter, Bush, and Clinton administrations—and how much more can be accomplished by the Obama administration.

INCLUSION IS A COMPONENT OF A NATIONAL INDUSTRIAL STRATEGY

The White House appointee would ensure that diverse businesses would be an essential component of the National Industrial Strategy that this country so urgently needs.[1]

Free-market mechanisms worked well in the isolated domestic markets of the past, but we are seeing that overreliance on them today can place nations at a disadvantage. We are competing in a global economy against rival nations that have their own national industrial strategies to guide and foster the development of competitive advantage in targeted industries. When other nations tilt the playing field to their advantage, a directionless free-market ideology constrains U.S. business success. As revenue streams, then jobs, then whole industry clusters migrate offshore, the need for a U.S. National Industrial Strategy becomes more urgent with each passing day.

We need a strong sense of direction to the national economy to preserve capitalism, not to undermine it. Look at recent history. The banking collapse of 2008 certainly required urgent steps to get the staggering economy back on its feet, but it resulted in a disconnected set of interventions. We can understand how that can happen in the midst of crisis, but we now realize that it is inefficient to simply pump cash into the system and hope that it is spent in a way that restores consumer confidence, keeps people in their homes, stimulates borrowing and spending, and generates the breadth of economic participation needed to restore nationwide prosperity.

It is irresponsible to be creating national debt obligations without having a national investment strategy. What the government spends will have to be repaid by our children and grandchildren, so the need for ex-

pedient action should not distract us from making a thoughtful investment in our future—and theirs. *We need to create tomorrow's opportunities as well as today's jobs.* We need to create the human capital to staff
growth industries. We need to make the importing of strategic resources
(such as petroleum or rare earths) a choice rather than an act of dependency. And we need to foster technological breakthroughs that will sustain
our security, well-being, environment, energy supply, and quality of life.

A National Industrial Strategy would provide focus and direction to
our economic development. It would tell us what businesses the United
States needs to retain or develop, what industrial clusters must surround
the focal businesses, where clusters need to be located, what infrastructure will be required to sustain the chosen domains of commerce, and
what cadre of educated professionals will be needed to make our key industries viable in the global economy. Our national competitive advantage will determine our future standard of living.

Articulating a National Industrial Strategy will answer questions
like: Should we be injecting capital to keep the U.S. automakers liquid?
Should import/export policy be designed to minimize the carbon consequences of importing goods that could be sourced locally? Should we
buy military hardware from foreign companies? Should we be outsourcing composites manufacturing to Asia? Should we use tax policy to stabi-
lize gasoline and diesel prices at a level that reduces dependence on im-
ported fossil fuels? Should offshoring be tax deductible when it results
in a concomitant loss of jobs in economically distressed regions of the
United States? Should immigration quotas and student visa limitations
be determined by workforce needs? These decisions can be made ad hoc,
following fierce, divisive debates—or worse, with little debate because
lobbyists' money has trumped the public interest—or, they can be made
wisely in the context of a U.S. National Industrial Strategy.

To reiterate: *the issue is not whether the United States ought to have
a centrally planned economy; the issue is whether the country ought to
have a sense of direction that will guide public policy at all levels.* Whatever we decide about particular industries, tax policies, balance of trade,
preservation of strategically important industries, and the environmental
impact of sourcing, we still need to deal with the most fundamental issue

affecting our future economic prosperity—how to foster a thriving entrepreneurial economy. Restoration and sustainment of prosperity require the
inclusion of the fastest-growing sector of the entrepreneurial economy—
the businesses owned by minorities and women.

THE GOAL IS TO DEVELOP SUCCESSFUL BUSINESSES

Entrepreneurs are independent thinkers and doers. They have high aspirations, high energy, a high rate of innovation—and a high rate of failure.
Figure 3.1[2] shows the expected attrition rate over the years. Many start-
ups are destined to fail within their first years. And note that these data
do not represent recession years, in which the attrition rate would be
vastly higher.

A large number of start-ups are ill conceived and *ought* to fail. That
sounds harsh, but selection mechanisms operate in business much as they
do in biology: the fittest survive; the unfit sooner or later disappear from
the population.

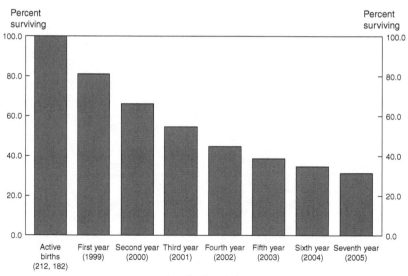

FIGURE 3.1

Survival of New Establishments from Second Quarter of 1998

The problem in an economic system arises when businesses that ought to succeed end up failing. If an entrepreneur has a good idea, customers exist that could benefit from commercialization of that idea, and wealth and jobs could be created if the supplier were to succeed, then it is in the public interest to give the entrepreneur an opportunity to bring the product or service to market.

In the case of diverse businesses, the opportunity is too often blocked. A useful and legitimate role of government is to help the diverse entrepreneur get beyond the blockage.

Historically, entrepreneurs from diverse backgrounds have run into three principal sources of blockage:

- Access to contracts
- Access to capital
- Business knowledge deficit

We will look at how minority business enterprises (MBEs) in particular are differentially affected by these barriers to success, and how government can promote their survival despite the system being somewhat stacked against them. We will show why it is *in the public interest* for government to take action that will create a different future for minorities—as well as for women—who want to be economically self-sufficient.

IMPROVING ACCESS TO CONTRACTS IS CHALLENGING
Governments can use their enormous purchasing and budget-allocation power to ensure that opportunities are made available to diverse suppliers. Their mandates require some of the public spending to result in business for minorities (as well as Native Americans, women, and veterans). But it is one thing to issue a mandate and another thing to achieve results.

Mandates require a behavioral change among purchasing agents, who are risk averse, for understandable reasons. If they do a good job, they are invisible (they are like the alternator in your car: although it is indispensible, if it is working well, you are unaware that it is there at all). If the purchasing department does a better job, people will give them no more recognition than a positive review at the end of the year. But if there is even a small supply disruption or quality problem, management turns a bright spotlight on them, and that is how the purchasing department gets remembered—as the group that jeopardized the smooth running of the organization. Because the cost of being wrong is high, purchasing agents have a natural tendency to stick with incumbent suppliers as long as they can.

But this tendency makes it difficult for any new supplier to get a foot in the door. And the difficulty is even greater for minorities and women, who might encounter stereotyping that induces some behind-the-times purchasing agents to assume that they will not get the same reliability, quality, or responsiveness if they deal with diverse suppliers.

INCLUSIVE OUTSOURCING MANDATES ARE GOOD FOR THE COUNTRY

Civil rights legislation discourages overt discrimination, and norms have emerged that make hateful stereotyping socially unacceptable in most of the country. But the absence of current discrimination does not proactively draw historically excluded people into the entrepreneurial economy where their contribution is urgently needed. That is why *programs to foster the participation of diverse employees and diverse suppliers were in the national interest when they were created and are still needed today.* Inclusionary contracting policies and programs create the extra push that is needed to overcome twin barriers: the traditional governmental standard-operating procedure of buying from the lowest bidder, and the risk-aversion bias of purchasing agents.

Of course, setting aside a small portion of the total purchase volume will always draw protests from incumbents and the good ol' boys. Those who object will not acknowledge having benefited from superior access to contracts but will bemoan losing something to which they feel entitled. But the chorus of protests from the privileged must not drown out the voice of reason. It is wise public policy to allocate a portion of contract volume to be spent in communities that are mired in persistent poverty or among members of groups that have faced past discrimination. It enables all citizens to contribute to gross domestic product, and it serves the common good.

Outsourcing mandates, sometimes called set-aside programs, have the purpose of breaking *the cycle of economic exclusion*. The cycle operates because diverse businesses do not get awarded current contracts because they do not have a track record; they do not have a track record because of past discrimination; and they will not get business in the future if they cannot create the track record they need today. Outsourcing mandates break this cycle, by giving historically excluded groups an opportunity to establish a track record. After being given a fair chance, it is up to the diverse businesses: if they perform well, they will have the experience and references to compete for future contracts; if they perform poorly, they will not. Providing access to contracts makes the uphill playing field a little more level.

It is likewise in the national interest to use outsourcing mandates to draw business into geographic areas that have a high poverty rate. It is well documented that minority businesses tend to hire minorities at a higher rate than whites do. So if we want to create economic self-sufficiency in inner cities, poor rural communities, or impoverished Indian reservations, then it makes sense to provide these communities with business opportunities: the alternative is to pay for unemployment compensation, welfare, public housing, stronger police forces, larger prison systems, more drug rehabilitation, and other remedial services.

The long-term benefits to community development are even more important than the short-term savings. By fostering the establishment of minority-owned businesses, we create positive role models in distressed communities. We want young people in inner cities to aspire to be tomorrow's entrepreneurs—and not tomorrow's gangstas, pimps, drug dealers, or muggers. They need to see that it is possible to be successful in the legitimate economy; they are already overexposed to the apparent success of inner-city people operating in the underground economy.

An especially compelling case for preference programs can be made when access to contracts involves local public-sector spending. Suppose a community is building a new school. Much of the cost will be borne by local taxpayers. If a locally owned business pays its share of local taxes and can do as good of a job as an out-of-town bidder, then isn't it appropriate to give the work to the local supplier? It is certainly in the public interest to do so. Local businesses obtain most of their supplies and labor locally, creating local jobs for people who spend their paychecks locally, and in turn creating a multiplier effect that boosts local tax revenues. It is a positive outcome for the community. The public interest is served.

In sum, it is in the public interest to require that any organization that receives money from a government—directly or indirectly, in the form of contracts, loans, loan guarantees, or other benefits—should be required to have an effective, impactful supplier diversity program in place that flows down through however many tiers there are in the value chain.

GOVERNMENTS NEED TO ENFORCE INCLUSION MANDATES

We cannot conclude this discussion of access to contracts without noting how inadequately these programs have been working in practice. Governmental entities almost universally fall short of their goals in directing outsourcing work to diverse businesses, most often due to managerial failures. Mandates specify the policy; accountability identifies who is responsible for implementing it; and control systems reward compliance and penalize noncompliance. This is Management 101, not rocket science. So why do inclusion mandates have such a dismal record of success?

Probably the biggest impediment is the resiliency of the outdated purchasing tradition. Many governments insist on getting three bids and buying from the lowest bidder, but they do not bother to ascertain whether this gets them the best value.

Suppose you are buying a commodity item such as bricks to build the new school, and you issue a statewide request for quotation. One bid comes in ridiculously high, another twice what Home Depot would charge, and a third so low the supplier would go out of business if the bid were accepted. Which one should the municipal purchasing agent take? The answer, of course, is "none of the above." This purchasing process is fundamentally flawed. It is a mechanism for completing a task, not a strategy for serving the public interest. The purchasing agent should, in this case, cancel the procurement and start again with an approach that creates real value. He or she would probably end up with a negotiated price from a local supplier that would keep the money in the community, minimize the carbon consequences of transportation, and keep the local supplier in business—to preserve local jobs and help ensure that there will be a local source in the coming years.

The aforementioned example shows that traditional public-sector purchasing may in practice be *contrary* to the public interest. Public officials should be evaluating standard operating procedures and debating *why* business should be given to the lowest bidder. Even if that practice minimizes public spending, it does not guarantee that taxpayers get maximum overall benefit. In practice, this process often results in a supplier underbidding to get the job, and then making up for the low bid by underdelivering or overcharging when the contract needs to be amended because of unanticipated "surprises."

Responsible public officials will recognize that "putting contracts out to bid" is in some cases a good idea, and in other cases a bad idea. They then can use their ingenuity to devise a legitimate, fair, auditable purchasing process that is tailored to each situation.

The inclusion mandate ought to make it easy for minority-owned enterprises to do business with the governmental organization. Standard operating procedures should not *have the effect of* blocking minority inclusion. For example, onerous paperwork that does not benefit the taxpayer should be eliminated, and long processing periods for applications, permits, bids, and invoicing should be streamlined. It is not difficult to discover the barriers to diverse participation: public officials can get all the information they need by holding a public meeting and asking what makes it difficult to do business with them. Most entrepreneurs will not be shy about telling them.

With barriers to participation removed, officials must assess incentive structures. If public officials and prime contractors make an effort to ensure minority inclusion, are they credited or rewarded for doing so? What are the penalties if they fall short of achieving public goals? If government creates a mechanism whereby it is in the decision makers' self-interest to achieve minority inclusion, they will find that people can be very resourceful in assuring success. If there are no penalties for ignoring public mandates, and no rewards for accomplishing them, then public officials have done no more than "hope for the best." That is not good enough.

LOBBYING CAN DERAIL DIVERSE ACCESS TO CONTRACTS

Women are already the majority of the U.S. population, and minorities are on their way to becoming the majority. So if government does what it is supposed to do—represent citizens' interests—then diverse businesses should have full access to contracts that directly or indirectly involve public funding. Yet women and minorities are not proportionally represented in public- or private-sector value chains, and there is little enforcement action when goals go unmet. How could this happen in America— the world's exemplar of equal opportunity?

In some third-world countries, rich business owners are able to bribe politicians to steer contracts their way, to stifle legislation that would create a level playing field, and to discourage enforcement of the legislation that does get passed. In those countries, there are tremendous wealth differentials between owners (and executives) of large businesses and the people who work for them or serve as suppliers. The wealth imbalance and opportunity imbalance are sustained by the cozy arrangement between politicians and business owners.

In the United States, it is against the law to bribe politicians to gain preferential treatment. But it is legal to make political campaign donations that create the same results as bribery. Our nation's "lobbying system" enables rich business owners to induce politicians to steer contracts their way, to stifle legislation that would create a level playing field, and to discourage enforcement of legislation that creates inclusion. Our system creates tremendous wealth differentials between owners (and executives) of large businesses and the people who work for them or serve as suppliers. The wealth imbalance and opportunity imbalance are sustained by the cozy arrangement between politicians and business owners, just as it is in third-world countries.

The current system of lobbying, though corrupt in its very essence, is deeply embedded in our political system—despite violating our values and working against the national interest. Thus an end to lobbyist control of public policy has been a central tenet of the promise of "Change We Can Believe In." The country is ready for the reform the public craves, and inclusion mandates will be more effectively implemented if politicians' motives are not compromised.

PUBLIC-SECTOR CERTIFICATION NEEDS REENGINEERING

Certification of diverse ownership is important. It is a mechanism designed to prevent fraud. It ensures that contracts that are intended for diverse enterprises are not being diverted to businesses that public policy was not intended to foster.

The need for certification exists because some people are unconstrained by ethics and are willing to misrepresent their business as having diverse ownership and management when it does not. They create "front" companies that seem to be minority owned or woman owned, but in fact they are majority owned or male owned. Examples of common abuses are

- using a minority company to bid for the business, sign the contract, and process the invoices, while adding no real economic value (or, in contract parlance, there is little "self-performed" work);
- legally registering a business in the wife's name so it appears to be a woman-owned and woman-operated business; and
- creating a business that "on paper" has 51 percent minority ownership but is majority operated, and where most of the profits are channeled to a large corporation or a white, male-owned company.

These arrangements are all fraudulent. To combat such abuses, the certification process, done properly, verifies that the business pursuing a contract opportunity is, indeed, a diverse business. It establishes who owns the business, who runs the business, and who gets the profits. It is not a uniform process, and various approaches are more or less effective in serving the public interest.

Self-certification is close to being no certification at all. It is nothing more than a claim that is not verified. It invites misrepresentation by unscrupulous business operators.

Public-sector certification can be thorough, but in many cases the certification has geographic recognition that is unreasonably limited. Some minority businesses, certified *by the state* as being legitimately diverse owned and operated, are required to obtain separate certification by some cities *within that state* as being minority owned. If one has state certification that verifies minority status and business address, one would think that any official in a city could pull out a map and ascertain that the city is within the state that has already certified the business! The same phenomenon occurs when national certification of minority status is not accepted at the state level.

One is left wondering why we do not yet have universal reciprocal certification in this country. Everyone—except some certifying authorities—is asking for it. Policy makers need to assess the burden being placed on diverse businesses: it is simply unfair to make them get certified multiple times. The diverse owners would be better off spending their time and efforts running their businesses and delivering real value to their customers.

The obvious solution, of course, is National Certification of diverse status. It would be a passport-quality certificate. The standards would be as high as those of any of the certifying authorities, and there would be significant penalties for fraudulent representations. The National Certification would cover minority group, gender, veteran status, city, state, and zip code. The certification would have to be updated, under penalty of law, after every change of address, ownership, or management. It would definitively ascertain eligibility for any public- or private-sector program. The zip codes of the business and its workforce would establish HUB Zone eligibility. The National Certification program could be administered by the nearest SBA office, or outsourced to a nonprofit agency. There is no excuse for not having this mechanism in place already.

GOVERNMENTS CAN IMPROVE ACCESS TO CAPITAL

Even before the credit crisis of 2008, minority entrepreneurs had difficulty obtaining start-up and working capital.

Before a business can start selling to customers, the entity may need to pay for its capital assets—such as a building, a franchise fee, a computer, machinery, or a fleet of vehicles. Later on, when incoming revenues are adequate, these initial business outlays can be gradually repaid. But at the outset, the typical minority business needs start-up capital.

Working capital is needed when the business is up and running. A business is profitable if at the end of the year the money taken in from sales exceeds the money paid out in expenses. The cash-flow problem, even for a highly profitable business, arises *during* the year. The entrepreneur has to pay for raw materials and infrastructure costs (rent, utilities, wages, insurance, etc.) up front but does not get paid by customers until thirty days after the job is completed. That thirty days is sometimes stretched to sixty days, ninety days, or even longer, depending on how badly the customer treats its vendors. And if the business is growing, the cash-flow challenge is more of a problem, because the growth must be financed by higher near-term outlays.

Additional working capital is needed when customers require the supplier to hold a large "safety stock" of inventory to accommodate surprises; the supplier usually has to finance that inventory and only gets paid for what gets sold. Even if such requirements do not significantly affect the profitability of the firm, they can create cash-flow problems.

CAPITAL AVAILABILITY DEPENDS
ON SOCIOECONOMIC STATUS

The most well-to-do entrepreneurs have enough money to finance the start-up, provide working capital, and bankroll growth: for such entrepreneurs, availability of capital is high, and cost of capital is low. They are more likely than not to come from affluent families that are socially connected to the business community. If they do not have enough start-up or working capital themselves, they may be able to borrow from family or friends. If these options fail, bankers will be predisposed to give them a fair hearing and possibly the benefit of the doubt, due to the exchange of favors (sometimes referred to as "professional courtesy") that happens in affluent social networks. Thus, in practice, business decisions are not quite as arm's length or economically rational as one might expect from reading all of the formulas and ratios presented in business textbooks.

Most minority entrepreneurs are not affluent, and rarely are they from wealthy families with strong social connections to financiers. Theirs is a different situation: on average, the net worth of minority families is less a small fraction—roughly one-tenth—of the net worth of their white counterparts.[3] So self-financing and family-backed financing are seldom adequate sources of capital for minority business owners.

The availability of bank loans depends on the entrepreneur's credit-worthiness. Financial data, business plans, and credit history are all inputs the loan officer will look at, but the decision is ultimately a judgment call: Will this creditor pay the interest when it comes due, and will the bank ever get its principal back? The bank has some hope of getting at least some of its money back if it holds collateral. An affluent white homeowner can take out a second mortgage, pledge retirement funds, or get well-to-do family members to guarantee loans. In contrast, minorities tend to rent, rather than own, their homes, and they are less likely to have other resources available that would be accepted as collateral.

Furthermore, minorities tend to gravitate toward service industries, where the capital asset requirements are low. This makes it easier to start up the business but more difficult to finance ongoing operations and growth. In a manufacturing business, the machinery and real estate may be used as collateral for a working capital loan, but a typical service business does not involve ownership of such assets. Minorities get trapped in one of those nasty cycles: they have to go into service businesses because they have no capital; then they cannot get capital because they are in a service business. The adage, "You need money to make money," has an ironic ring to it: minorities need money, but they rarely have it.

So let's go back to that loan officer who has to make a judgment call. Judgments are made on the basis of data and assumptions, but both are subject to human biases. The result is that, for whatever reasons, minorities and women find it harder to get loans approved and pay higher borrowing costs than their white male counterparts.[4] This does not mean that we should try to punish biased loan decisions. Bias is hard to prove in each particular case and may be unconscious on the part of loan officers. Instead, we should amend public policy so that we provide affordable alternative sources of capital, otherwise many diverse businesses will have to resort to high-cost debt.

High-cost debt has been a temptation for desperate entrepreneurs because the underregulated financial services industry has been careless—sometimes even cavalier—in its issuance of credit cards. In recent years, some people received multiple unsolicited credit cards in the mail every month. The temptation for desperate entrepreneurs to use the cards is enormous, but the cost of using them can be equally enormous, with many banks charging an effective interest rate exceeding 20 percent. Minorities and many women need better alternatives in accessing the capital they need to run their businesses.

GOVERNMENTS SHOULD PROVIDE DIRECT ACCESS TO CAPITAL

Government purchasing agents are invariably in a better cash position than most small businesses. So if it is in the public interest to promote the survival of a diverse supply chain, then *governments and their prime contractors should be paying their diverse suppliers on favorable terms*. Some governmental units pay diverse businesses within fifteen days of receiving an accurate invoice. Some even pay by debit or credit card, so that the supplier gets immediate access to the sales revenue. But some other governmental units drive their diverse suppliers to the brink of liquidity and beyond.

We discussed cash flow first, because it tends to be a leading cause of failure among entrepreneurial business. But all ongoing enterprises need to be adequately capitalized, and this can be a big challenge for minority businesses. Capital structure is equity plus debt, and the ability to secure ongoing financing depends on the balance between the two. Minorities that have too much debt already cannot get additional loans.

Governments can help minorities attract equity investment by providing tax incentives, or by assuring investors that the business in which they take an equity position will be provided with a public-sector revenue stream if it is run well and if it delivers value.

Those same governments have a greater range of options in providing debt financing. They can guarantee loans, limiting the bank's risk and its consequent aversion to lending to minorities who may be perceived as high risk. But they cannot force lending institutions to make loans if they do not want to extend the credit. So governments must provide alternative financing mechanisms to address situations where it is in the public interest to have the diverse business get the capital it needs. In such cases, it is best to provide low-interest loans directly, without having an intermediary lending institution in the loop. But other creative solutions ought to be considered, such as by pooling the risk in a loan fund dedicated to financing minority businesses.

THE CONSTRUCTION INDUSTRY HAS HIGH POTENTIAL FOR MINORITY PARTICIPATION

The biggest opportunity to foster MBE success has been in the construction industry. This is an industry where minority participation is feasible due to low barriers to entry (capital requirements are generally low, MBEs do not need specialized education, and learning curves tend to be steep and manageable). Yet a very real barrier to entry is raised when they are denied surety bonding.

Consider the example of a city that authorizes a $100 million public works project. The project authorization includes the stipulation that 25 percent of the construction be done by local, small, disadvantaged business enterprises. The intent is to foster the growth of local construction firms so that local jobs will be created and the community's money will be re-spent and retained in the local economy. This creates a $25 million opportunity for the set of disadvantaged construction firms in the city. But the Miller Act (dating back to 1935) and its state and local clones require that construction firms post a surety bond if their contract exceeds $100,000. So only the minority-owned construction firms that have the financial resources to post large bonds are eligible to participate. Because, historically, minorities—and women—have been excluded from the construction industry, few diverse businesses have accumulated the resources that would enable them to post the bonds. As a result, the firms that were intended to get the business are barred by law from bidding.

If the city government is sincere about achieving minority participation—and creating capacity for future minority involvement in major construction projects—then city officials can use their ingenuity to set up the city's own surety bonding mechanism, without any involvement of the private-sector surety bonding "establishment." The only barrier is ideological, yet governments provide other public services— defense, policing, welfare, weather forecasting, research, health care, and so on—so why not surety bonding? Doing so would facilitate inclusion of groups that would otherwise be denied access to an important industry with low barriers to entry.

Public bonding is not the only solution. Financiers ought to be able to come up with a surety arrangement that will work for the benefit of MBEs. The recent proliferation of novel financing instruments on Wall Street testifies to how creative financial experts can be when they want to address a challenge.

KEY MANAGEMENT SKILLS CAN BE DEVELOPED EASILY

Recall from Chapter 1 that disadvantaged groups are most likely to have educational deficits. This is a consequence of not learning much in locally financed school systems that are starved for resources in poor neighborhoods. Aspiring business owners in these communities tend to have little opportunity for mentoring from entrepreneurs in their extended families, due to past discrimination against preceding generations. The result is a business knowledge deficit. Public-sector entities at all levels that are concerned with economic development need to supplement entrepreneurs' education with remedial or supportive learning experiences.

When large corporations have a knowledge deficit, they hire people who have the qualifications, they train current workers so that they develop the requisite knowledge, or they hire consultants on a project basis. Fledgling businesses can have similar needs, but they often lack the financial resources to exercise any of these options. It is in the public interest to provide management and technical assistance to businesses that have the potential to benefit from it.

Entrepreneurs, as we have noted earlier, tend to know more about manufacturing a product or delivering a service than they know about *running* a business. When fledgling businesses fail, it is rarely because the entrepreneurs could not do the work tasks properly; it is almost always because they mismanaged the enterprise. Usually, the business owner has made avoidable errors.

So if we as a nation want a healthy entrepreneurial economy, we need to make an investment in training people not to make common mistakes—such as overlooking cash-flow problems, taking on business they cannot handle, ignoring customer preferences, growing too fast, failing to set up control systems, or putting all of their eggs in one basket by overreliance on a single dominant customer. We have found that even just a week of intensive training can save most entrepreneurs from learning lessons the hard way—which often involves financial ruin.

The SBA has recognized the wisdom of investing in the success of high-potential disadvantaged business: its 7(j) program is designed to provide the management and technical assistance that often makes the difference between survival and failure. But this program has been cut, along with the other resources that the SBA needs to be effective. We will say more about the demise of the 7(j) program when we consider how the SBA can most advantageously be restored as a fully functioning agency.

FEDERAL GOVERNMENTAL SUPPORT HAS BEEN AD HOC AND INSUFFICIENT

In the past few decades, we have had different governmental units serving business subgroups, with some diverse businesses getting no attention at all, and others getting incomplete service from multiple sources. Here are some examples to illustrate the inadequate coverage of minority business needs.

Minorities

Minority-owned businesses are the primary responsibility of the MBDA, created by executive order and situated within the U.S. Department of Commerce. It is the only governmental unit charged with the specific mission of promoting the success of minority-owned businesses. Minority businesses are also served by several SBA programs, including HUB Zone, 8(a), and 7(j) programs. The U.S. Department of Agriculture (USDA) also has several outreach programs to stimulate economic activity in minority-dominated poor rural communities. There are more than 4 million minority-owned businesses in the United States. Budgets are so low and personnel so few that less than 1 percent of these businesses are being helped to succeed.

Native Americans

Indian reservations are sovereign nations within the U.S. borders that have treaties with the U.S. government. The Bureau of Indian Affairs within the Department of Interior is responsible for the welfare of American Indian tribes, implementing treaty obligations. But Native Americans have never been happy with the support they receive from this agency. Today, the vitality of reservation economies is supported by the Office of Indian Energy and Economic Development (OIEED), which is responsible for providing assistance *when requested* to tribally owned businesses and Native-owned businesses operating on Indian reservations.

Outside of the reservations, Native Americans are considered minorities and are served by the Office of Native American Business Development, U.S. Department of Commerce—a congressionally mandated but as yet not fully funded office that has been temporarily housed within the MBDA. The SBA also has had a skeletal Office of Native American Affairs. And the USDA has several outreach programs to foster economic activity on tribal lands.

Alaska Natives are included in the general category of Native Americans and are served by all of the aforementioned governmental units, even though their situations are unique and, in many cases, their communities are on the brink of starvation. The peculiar challenge in sustaining village economies in America's only Arctic state is their remoteness and isolation. Economic development programs that are barely adequate for most Native Americans are simply inapplicable to most of the landmass of Alaska.

Veterans

Veteran-owned businesses are served primarily by the Veterans Administration (VA), which has a Center for Veterans Enterprise. Veteran businesses are also served by the Office of Veterans Business Development

(OVBD) within the SBA. There are 3 million veteran-owned businesses in the United States, being served by ten specialists in the OVBD and ten specialists in the SBA. Service-disabled veterans do not typically have special needs when they operate entrepreneurial businesses, but the country has a special obligation to help them succeed: they have made a sacrifice for their country that the nation needs to repay.

Women

The SBA has an Office of Women's Business Ownership that has an outreach operation comprising more than one hundred Women's Business Centers, each with two or three consultants and a budget in the low-six figures. Many of them are mandated to also serve entrepreneurs in other traditionally underrepresented categories, which dilutes their emphasis on the special needs of fledgling women-owned enterprises. The number of centers sounds impressive until one realizes that there are 8 million women-owned business enterprises in the United States. That means, on average, that these small centers would each have to serve nearly 80,000 women-owned business enterprises (WBEs). In general, women have very high potential to be successful business owners and operators, and they are the demographic majority. It is in the public interest to foster their full participation in the economic system.[5]

THE NEED IS GREAT, THE SUPPORT
SYSTEM INADEQUATE

By the end of 2008, the United States was in the deepest recession since the Great Depression, with economists predicting a slow recovery lasting many years. The restoration of economic vitality depends on the success of the entrepreneurial sector. Small business is the driving force of the U.S. economy: it is the primary source of job creation and wealth creation, and it generates the multiplier effect, whereby earned money gets spent and re-spent several times. The entrepreneurial sector also fuels the economic growth engine that drives tomorrow's economy: the Googles, Wal-Marts, Apples, Home Depots, and Microsofts were yesterday's start-ups; they grew to take the place of yesterday's blue-chip companies, such as U.S. Steel, RCA, Kodak, Xerox, and DEC. Thus the success of the entrepreneurial sector determines both the short-term and long-term prosperity of the nation.

The economic system has some things in common with Mother Nature: for a population to flourish, many young have to survive the early years when they are most vulnerable, otherwise they never get the chance to prove themselves in the harsh world of competition and predation. Governments need to help potentially viable disadvantaged businesses for the same reasons we immunize children against known health hazards.

Our urban centers and poor rural communities need to flourish, or at least be economically self-sufficient. So do our Indian reservations. Our National Guards and Reserves need to re-create the businesses they had to abandon in order to serve tours of duty for their country; likewise, servicemen and servicewomen being discharged from active duty need to be contributing to gross domestic product rather than adding to the ranks of the unemployed, so that those who aspire to be entrepreneurs should be given all of the help we can muster in making that transition successful. And women who have entrepreneurial ambitions need to make their full contributions to the economic system.

We need to help all of these current or potential business owners get past the most vulnerable phase of their business life cycles and achieve what they are capable of achieving. But our current approach to providing the necessary support has been piecemeal and insufficient.

WE MUST DO A BETTER JOB OF LEVERAGING EXISTING RESOURCES

Government programs at various levels can and should make a difference in the survival, prosperity, and growth to scale of its businesses owned by minorities and other historically disadvantaged groups. The biggest difference will come at the federal level, but states must also have programs. These may be smaller-scale "clones" of federal programs, but they can be fine-tuned to nurture industry clusters suited to their particular geographies, resource bases, or locations. Local programs are extremely important too, particularly where there are large concentrations of minorities, deep poverty, dominant industries in decline, or unique opportunities.

Federal programs will have the greatest overall impact, but they are in dire need of improvement. There has been needless duplication of effort with multiple agencies serving the same economic subgroup, none of them doing a particularly good job, and a lack of cooperation and coordination between them.

Wasteful, ineffective spending needs to be eliminated: nobody disputes that, especially now. Federal budgets are tight, due to wartime spending without wartime taxing, an ad hoc program of paying for the mistakes of banking industry executives, an urgent, desperate, and largely unfocused program to spend money in the quest for economic stimulus, and a tax code that is biased toward the rich.

It is time to stop settling for piecemeal solutions and develop a comprehensive inclusion strategy that achieves economic impact, creates jobs, and drives out inefficiencies. We list some elements of a short-term strategy that would be a lot more effective than what we currently have in place, and we then reiterate the need for strong leadership.

THE SBA NEEDS TO BE REBUILT

The capacity of the SBA was cut back during the last two decades. Its capacity needs to be restored and its administrator elevated to Cabinet-level status. The SBA's primary role has been to guide small businesses through the *start-up* phase. Small start-ups have common needs, whether they are owned by white males, minorities, veterans, women, Native Americans, or anyone else. The most important function of the SBA is to help entrepreneurs create a viable, disciplined, and comprehensive business plan.

There are standard operating procedures for helping people create a start-up plan. Filling out a business plan forces the dreamer to assess the factors that will determine his or her success or failure. Many people, upon discovering all of the things they need to do to operate a successful business, decide against becoming entrepreneurs. In such cases, the SBA does them a service by making apparent what entrepreneurs are "in for" before they give up their day jobs and squander their family savings. And the ones that persevere have a plan for surviving the multiple challenges of the start-up phase.

As resources have been withdrawn from the SBA, the teaching and coaching that the agency once provided have been largely eliminated. To the SBA's credit, its Web-based tools have been improved considerably. But here is the problem: the people who most need help—denizens of inner cities, barrios, and Indian reservations—seldom have the level of education or computer literacy to use Web-based tools. Many of them do not own a computer, have no access to broadband if they did have a computer, and do not have anyone in the family who has the technological acumen to help out. Yet these are people who may have a powerful entrepreneurial drive, the ability to form positive relationships with customers, a strong work ethic, and good ideas. They could be successful if provided with adequate SBA education and coaching.

The money that the SBA once allocated for management and technical assistance has evaporated. In 2007, the SBA budget for training minorities, under the 7(j) program, was only $2 million. Put this in perspective: there are more than 4 million minority businesses in the United States and the SBA allocated $2 million to invest in their training to be successful entrepreneurs. Now do the math: that means the country invested an average of fifty cents in the success of each minority business. So there was essentially no money for education; and, after an 80 percent drawdown in personnel, there were not many people available for operating any of the SBA's support services.

The SBA has been more helpful in the realm of providing loan guarantees (which involves having commercial lending institutions such as banks issue loans, but reducing their risk by compensating them for most of their loss in the case of defaults). It is generally agreed that it is in the public interest to have minorities take on the challenge of running businesses in economically depressed communities. Their entrepreneurial enterprises make goods and services locally available, keep money recirculating in the community, provide jobs or at least role models, and keep a family self-employed that otherwise might have been on welfare (or participating in the underground economy, incurring a whole set of so-cial and economic costs). Economic self-sufficiency is an important com-ponent of community development and the nation's urban strategy.

Now let's shift our perspective from the public interest to the local bank's interest. The bank loan officers looking at the business plans—even in the absence of any biases based on racial or gender stereotyping—might perceive high risk in making the loan to an inner-city business. And they might want repayment in time periods that are shorter than the entrepreneur can comfortably manage. They probably want to get loans repaid soon so the money can be loaned out again, earning new fees, and avoid having the bank's funds remain at risk. Thus it might be *in the bank's interest* to deny the loan, but it may be *in the public interest* to accept higher risks and longer payback periods than the bank is willing to take.

In such circumstances, the SBA performs a useful role by reducing the bank's risk exposure, but if the bank has better investment opportunities, it may not want to make loans to minorities even when the downside risk is limited. A program of direct loans would make more sense. It would enable the high-potential entrepreneur to get the needed financing and increase her or his opportunity to succeed.

The SBA also serves the public interest by operating the HUB Zone program. This program encourages outsourcing to small businesses in Historically Underutilized Business Zones—areas with chronically de-pressed incomes or high unemployment. The program requires the busi-nesses to employ a significant number of local residents, which creates jobs and circulates money in the depressed local economy. This successful SBA program ought to be tightly integrated with the strategy of other governmental units, such as the Economic Development Agency, within the U.S. Department of Commerce.

The SBA also plays a useful role in administering the 8(a) Business Development Programs. The objective is to nurture the development of firms owned and controlled at least 51 percent by economically or socially disadvantaged individuals. The concept is to help entrepreneurs learn to do business with the federal sector—the nation's largest customer—without creating perpetual dependency on preferential access. So the program allows for four years of development during which the disadvantaged entrepreneur is somewhat sheltered from competition, followed by a five-year transition period during which the business has to become robust enough to compete in the open market. The U.S. economy benefits from broader economic inclusion and increased competition among competent suppliers.

All of the SBA's programs thus serve the national interest, and not just the interests of population subgroups. The agency's current weaknesses stem from repeated ideologically motivated, lobbyist-influenced attempts to eliminate it. Fortunately, the agency has survived, and its capacity can be restored to fulfill its important mission. But the rebuilding will take time.

When the SBA is restored, the agency needs to maximize the effectiveness of its decentralized network of satellite field offices that serves local business communities. The people staffing these Small Business Development Centers (SBDCs) need to be trained in a uniform, systematic approach to helping businesses in the early phases of their life cycles. These centers' effectiveness depends totally on the quality of SBDC human capital.

- Coaching is the centers' most impactful function. SBDC personnel need to help promising entrepreneurs prepare business plans, loan applications, and certification paperwork. And they need to arrange mentoring relationships when feasible and appropriate.

- Second in importance is facilitating access to contracts. Desperate entrepreneurs often grab at straws, responding to RFQs whether it is a realistic opportunity or not. SBA personnel can help them focus their efforts on responding to RFQs for which they can realistically compete and avoid wasting their time on proposals that will never succeed.

- Third in importance is helping the growing business gain access to capital. This involves providing advice about desirable capital structure (the proportion of debt they ought to be carrying); explaining the various sources of financing and pointing out the pluses and minuses of each; teaching entrepreneurs how to complete loan application paperwork; and providing loan or bond guarantees when no other option is being made available. The time, energy, and resources of SBDC staff are necessarily going to be limited, so their efforts need to be leveraged. The SBA already accomplishes this to some degree by using volunteers from the SCORE (Service Corps of Retired Executives) program. But SBA offices need to be held accountable for collaborating closely with every other organization that can contribute to their effectiveness: other governmental agencies, nonprofits serving small business (chambers of commerce, advocacy organizations, NMSDC and Women's Business Enterprise National Council [WBENC] affiliates, etc.), business schools, and local schools willing to promote entrepreneurship among young people. It is not enough to have made an effort; the SBDCs need to achieve impact.

The SBA could be doing more to provide the training that diverse businesses need to survive beyond the start-up phase. But the knowledge needed by business owners at this stage of the business life cycle is not effectively achieved through distance learning, as noted earlier. The objective is to accelerate the development of the owners' judgment, so they can make wise decisions within their specific business contexts. This requires face-to-face ("classroom") learning experiences in which their own business is the case study, supplemented by individual coaching as necessary. The per-business cost is higher than for distance learning, but the number of businesses that have become established is much lower than the number of dreamers.

In sum, *the SBA should be as concerned with small business survival as it is with small business establishment.* And its programs and budget need to reflect this strategic mission.

THE MINORITY BUSINESS DEVELOPMENT AGENCY
NEEDS TO BE RESTRUCTURED
The MBDA, located within the Department of Commerce, traces its origins to the Nixon administration. It was designed to accelerate the eco-

nomic self-sufficiency of minorities—primarily urban African Americans at the outset—during the post-segregation era. It was at one time well funded, with a large number of field offices (Minority Business Enterprise Centers [MBECs]) around the country. The efforts were coordinated following the typical bureaucratic approaches of the day, with a Washington headquarters operation and regional offices in New York, Atlanta, Dallas, Chicago, and San Francisco.

The MBDA's budget has been cut repeatedly, especially during the past two decades. This funding trend is paradoxical, because the number of minority firms has grown dramatically. Yet by the end of 2008, the number of MBECs had been cut by more than half, with their budget allocations so meager that it would be difficult to hire and retain qualified business advisors. As a result, the MBDA became viewed as a top-heavy bureaucratic organization with an archaic regional office structure that consumed resources that could have been used instead to help minority businesses.

To the MBDA's credit, the agency had adjusted its mission to focus on helping established, high-growth potential minority businesses, and it left the start-ups for the SBA to handle. The rationale was that only a small percentage of minority businesses are large enough to create significant wealth and jobs in their communities. With decreasing resources available, narrowing the scope to achieve the greatest economic impact was a wise move.

Furthermore, the MBDA maximized its impact by allying with a major business school to train its contracted field operations staff as consultants and financial advisors, and to select its highest-potential minority entrepreneurs to attend one-week intensive learning experiences. But there is only so much that can be accomplished by an agency that has been systematically starved for resources. The MBDA can be retasked, restored, reengineered, or reinvented.

Retasking involves narrowing the MBDA's mission to gain the greatest impact with the limited resources available. Creating impact involves helping MBEs develop the capacity to create real value for major customers in the public and private sectors, and the scale to serve large customers efficiently. As we noted in the previous chapter, capacity has been achieved when the MBE can deliver on its value proposition in a way that creates competitive advantage—that is, when there is a reason for giving business to the MBE beyond philanthropy or sympathy. Scale results from organic growth, acquisition, or strategic alliance formation.

In the past, the MBDA has focused primarily on organic growth, which is a long, slow process for most businesses, with hitting a plateau the most likely outcome. To help MBEs achieve scale in the near term, the MBDA would have to facilitate acquisitions and strategic alliances—which would require the skill set characteristic of consultants, investment bankers, and venture capitalists. Success in retasking would require replacing many of the MBEC staff with people qualified for the new role. It would also involve transforming the regional bureaucracy into a set of consulting centers, largely copying the organizational structures of the major consulting firms.

Restoration involves providing the MBDA with enough resources to serve minority-dominated communities—say, fifty of the most-needy urban areas in the United States, plus some of the poor rural communities that have large concentrations of minorities. The efforts of a restored MBDA ought to be closely coordinated with those of the Economic Development Administration, a sister unit within the Department of Commerce.

The Washington MBDA headquarters would administer the contracts with MBECs but would provide enough funding to enable staffing by consultants with stronger qualifications. The MBDA would arrange continuing education for all of the client-facing field personnel. Operators of the MBECs would be held accountable for collaborating to the fullest extent with SBA offices and every other resource that would increase the impact on the population being served. The redundant regional offices would be eliminated to free up funding for higher-quality consultants. And the Washington headquarters office would specialize in helping larger MBEs secure national-level contracts.

Reengineering involves changing the process by which the MBDA services its target clients. MBDA employees would staff a small minority business referral center in each of the most-needy urban and rural areas.

Many of these could be collocated in existing SBA offices, since the referral centers are largely "virtual" offices with little demand for space other than occasional access to meeting rooms. Each referral center would assess needs and outsource services to the best provider. The referral center would also help the MBE make connections with potential customers, suppliers, bankers, or strategic alliance partners.

Financial advisors would be assigned to help each referral center serve its MBE clients. Many minority-owned businesses deserve loans or investment capital, but they lack the know-how to gain access to what is available. The MBDA has a strong history of being able to help these businesses when it has the financial experts available, but its budget has been so severely constrained during the past decade that the agency has not been able to afford to pay financing experts to work with the MBECs.

The referral center would leverage all of the resources that could make a difference to minority business enterprises. It would connect minority entrepreneurs with state and local government programs and opportunities. It would work collaboratively with the SBA office and its associated SCORE program. It would coordinate closely with the various chambers of commerce and advocacy groups. And it would mobilize the resources of the higher-education institutions to provide MBA consulting teams or interns. It could arrange mentor-protégé relationships for fledgling minority enterprises, and it could seek out technology-transfer opportunities so that minority businesses could reap the commercial benefits of developments in federal laboratories.

Reinvention involves a fundamental transformation in the present arrangements for serving disadvantaged businesses. The logic for this change is that established entrepreneurial businesses owned by minorities, women, and veterans have a lot in common. They have all faced historical discrimination; they have common characteristics and common challenges, and in many cases they have common opportunities. It is a public duty to streamline government while improving essential services, so here is an opportunity to do both.

The MBDA could be retasked, reengineered, and restructured to become the Diverse Business Development Agency (DBDA). It could be a unit within the reincarnated SBA, or it could remain within the U.S. Department of Commerce, perhaps as a subunit of the Economic Development Administration. Wherever it was housed, the DBDA would have a structure more like that of a professional consulting firm. It would operate a decentralized network of management consultants and financial advisors to provide tailored assistance to *established* businesses owned by minorities, women, and veterans, thereby complementing the work of the SBA, which specializes in helping start-ups.

Finally, the nation has not fulfilled its obligations to Native Americans. The obligations are explicit and arise primarily from treaties that the nation has repeatedly broken. The plight of most Indian communities is desperate—with unemployment often exceeding 50 percent, and chronic poverty, incarceration, drug and alcohol dependency, and epidemic abuse being more the norm than the exception in these communities. Yet the major federal agencies (Interior, Commerce, and the SBA) are simply not doing enough in Indian Country. This nation needs to create an effective, comprehensive program of economic support for its aboriginal peoples, and the program probably cannot succeed without a White House mandate and high-level design and coordination from the Department of Commerce.

A TRANSFORMATIONAL CHANGE WOULD BE IDEAL

In an ideal world, we would be starting with a blank sheet of paper, designing a system perfectly suited to helping minorities and other historically disadvantaged businesses start and operate their own businesses. If that were our assignment, we would probably integrate all of the disparate agencies serving small business within a redesigned governmental unit. The new entity could be the next evolutionary incarnation of the SBA, or it could be a unit of the U.S. Department of Commerce. It would be a broad-scope Business Development Agency (the USBDA), headed by a Cabinet-level administrator.

Wherever it was situated within the government, the USBDA would do everything the SBA now does, and more. The USBDA would have a decentralized hub-and-spoke network of units providing management consulting, financial advice, and loan and surety bond guarantees. Each unit would have programs tailored to the unique needs of various business categories with common challenges. Large businesses could be served by the hub. Medium-size businesses would be served by regional units, with an emphasis on fostering the global competitive advantage of American industry clusters. Small businesses would be served by decentralized offices. Start-ups would be served at the local level, providing self-paced Web-based assistance supplemented by face-to face instruction and coaching for entrepreneurs who need a person in the loop.

Specialized help would be provided to business owners who have special needs. The premier consulting firms have developed teams around industry clusters, and the USBDA could learn from their success in organizing themselves this way. For example, energy, aerospace, government contracting, construction, and health care are very different industries where industry knowledge is very important. General business knowledge is always necessary but is not sufficient for success in a particular sector of the business world. And general business knowledge is broadly available, so there is less of a need for the USBDA to provide it.

The USBDA would serve various client groups with special needs, therefore, it will need to have a matrix form. Minorities, women, Native Americans, veterans, residents of distressed urban areas, Alaska Natives, Puerto Ricans, entrepreneurs in poor rural areas, and Pacific Islanders all have special needs. They all face special challenges that would not be experienced by affluent white male college graduates operating their businesses in places like Silicon Valley, Manhattan, or Austin. America needs all of these businesses to be successful if all of the components of the economy are to pull together to create national prosperity. Specialized help consists of programs designed to address their unique needs and advisors who know how to maximize the business success of the particular groups.

But transformational change is just a dream. We need pragmatic, immediate solutions to immediate problems. So we have to make the best of what we have in place.

LEADERSHIP MUST COME FROM THE WHITE HOUSE

The evolution in government agencies that we need is broad in scope and deep in impact. That is why real progress will require the appointment of a White House *Special Assistant to the President for Diverse Business*. That person's mission would be to align Cabinet-level directives with economic stimulus initiatives, the long-term economic strategy, economic development, disaster recovery, and the urban strategy. The role would involve eliminating duplication, achieving demonstrable impact, resolving the "turf" disputes that inevitably arise between agencies, ensuring that government mandates are actually being carried out, and demanding interagency collaboration.

The leader's role would be to influence policies and practices beyond, as well as within, the realm of government. Most importantly, corporations would be persuaded to emphasize development over procurement in their supplier diversity programs, and territorial disputes among support organizations would be resolved so that they could collaborate to develop uniform, reciprocal certification. The Special Assistant to the President would promote and implement the overall strategy of economic inclusion and chair an advisory council to enable diverse voices to be heard when national-level policy was being formulated.

The public has embraced the promise of "Change We Can Believe In" and gave the administration the mandate to implement it. The change the public expects includes greater program effectiveness, greater government efficiency, and greater wealth creation among the economic classes whose purchasing power has been steadily eroding. In the latter category, minorities, Native Americans, women, and service-disabled veterans are overrepresented. They need help to achieve the American Dream.

High expectations were created. The Obama administration ran on a campaign of hope that was very successful: it *created* hope among those whose aspirations had been beaten down by years of disappointment, hopelessness, and despair. Now we need to deliver on the promise of change. We need a leader to be empowered to develop the entrepreneurial economy. He or she would assign clear and distinct roles to the various agencies; focus on achieving real inclusion, not just the token involvement we have been seeing; hold appointed officials accountable for both the impact of their own agencies and the success of their collaboration with other agencies; and manage relationships with the Congressional Caucuses.

In sum, someone good needs to be in charge of implementing an *inclusive* National Industrial Strategy. And to be effective, the person will need to be backed by the power and prestige of the White House to create the change the country needs.

4

CORPORATIONS SHOULD
REFOCUS ON DEVELOPMENT,
NOT PROCUREMENT

EXECUTIVE SUMMARY

In the new millennium, corporations rely heavily on outsourcing through a multitier supply chain and a distribution chain. Modern competition pits a corporation's value chain against rival value chains. So developing supplier excellence is an investment in the corporation's own competitive advantage.

With changing demographics, it is inevitable that diverse businesses will become an increasingly large component of corporate value chains. This makes supplier diversity a strategic priority, not a corporate citizenship obligation. In that context, the role of supplier diversity professionals is to ensure that diverse suppliers become not only as good as they can be but, quite literally, world class—because that is the standard against which minority business enterprises (MBEs) must compete for the business being outsourced today.

Supplier diversity professionals have seldom made a good case for their own strategic importance, often because they have not been positioned in that role. Instead, many are added to a traditional purchasing group with an assignment to modify outsourcing decisions so that the corporation accomplishes its goals for diversity-spend. But getting purchasing agents to deviate from long-established standard operating procedures is never an easy task. Without hierarchical power—and without articulating a compelling business case—the challenge facing supplier diversity professionals has been all uphill.

Not surprisingly, the results have been weak. American-based corporations have not integrated diverse suppliers into their value chains in proportion to their presence in the population. Many corporations make no effort at all, and of those that do make an effort, few achieve significant overall impact on the minority business community. The mediocre results are attributable not to a lack of effort and commitment from supplier diversity professionals but, rather, to the outdated procurement approach of many corporations.

Old-school purchasing is tactical rather than strategic: it focuses on procurement cost/benefit rather than on competitive advantage. Its standard operating procedures consist of announcing requirements, assessing supplier qualifications, soliciting bids, and choosing the best value-for-money. Supplier diversity is an add-on subprocess and tends to be resented as an operating constraint. It sets goals for a percentage of purchase volume to be placed with diverse suppliers, more often than not involving goods and services that are peripheral to the core value chain.

Success is sometimes assessed in terms of diversity-spend (accounts payable to diverse suppliers), impact on corporate image, and, among the most recalcitrant corporations, averting negative publicity generated by aggressive watchdog groups.

Advocacy/certification organizations reinforce the old-school paradigm and celebrate compliance rather than success. It is therefore possible to be honored for doing well when the corporation is in fact achieving very little impact. This leads to complacency with today's limited results, even though everyone concurs that corporations are not doing nearly enough.

Purchasing has evolved to the point that in leading-edge corporations, buyers do not place purchase orders; they manage outsourcing. Supplier diversity needs to evolve in parallel, otherwise supplier diversity professionals are doomed to be seen—and treated—as strategically irrelevant. They deserve better.

Supplier diversity needs to focus on value-chain *development* in the quest for competitive advantage rather than on modifying old-school *procurement* in the quest to achieve diversity-spend targets.

Leading-edge outsourcing identifies value-chain roles where diverse suppliers can meaningfully participate, recruits diverse businesses with the highest potential for long-term value creation, and then marshals the full spectrum of corporate resources to develop suppliers' capacity.

The rationale for providing support is strategic and self-interested: outsource partners are substitutes for in-house operations, therefore, it make sense to treat suppliers the same way the corporation would treat its own strategic business units and its own employees.

Leading-edge supplier diversity success is measured in terms of impact, which is positive when a diverse supplier has increased its *capacity to create real value*. If the diverse business does not become more of a strategic asset, then all the supplier diversity operation accomplishes is hitting a procurement quota.

The supplier diversity movement was established more than a quarter century ago, and its basic processes were attuned to the purchasing practices of the day. Since then, outsourcing processes have evolved to become strategic supply chain management, but supplier diversity processes are still largely geared to the old purchasing paradigm. As a result, supplier diversity does not get the recognition or cooperation it needs.

It is time for new thinking, new leadership, and new approaches.

CORPORATIONS SHOULD REFOCUS ON DEVELOPMENT, NOT PROCUREMENT

During much of the twentieth century, the major competitive arena was the domestic marketplace. Large corporations fought for domestic market share against other large corporations. They sometimes had "international divisions"—subunits that ran a secondary business selling outside of the domestic market. They were multinationals rather than global companies.

These corporations tended to be vertically integrated, which means they performed as much of the value-added work as possible in-house. The goal was to maximize control and capture profit from each link in the value chain. A mid-twentieth-century American example would be Ford competing against General Motors and Chrysler, primarily in the North

American market. Each company did most of its own components manufacturing.

The business world had changed considerably by the end of the twentieth century. Global corporations were now competing for worldwide market share, and vertical integration had been largely replaced by selective outsourcing.

The rationale for outsourcing is based on the general principle of comparative advantage. Instead of capturing every last opportunity for profit, corporations give up activities that value-chain partners can do better. Corporations retain "in house" the business activities that are strategically vital—contributions to value that take advantage of their core competency, and that produce a positive return on investment. All other activities are candidates for outsourcing to the best suppliers. A new-century example would be the major auto companies now outsourcing about two-thirds of the value of a vehicle.

As a result of this evolution of business practices, it is old-fashioned to think of corporations competing against rival corporations. Today, one integrated value chain competes against another integrated value chain. To continue the automotive example, Ford, allied with Ford's suppliers and go-to-market partners, competes against Toyota, allied with Toyota's suppliers and go-to-market partners.

Thus in the new millennium, the nature of competition has changed. It is the best value chain that wins.

So in today's marketplace, competitive advantage can come from anywhere in the value chain, often from outside the major corporation. A computer manufacturer may gain competitive advantage because of an innovation by a chip supplier. A consumer goods company may gain competitive advantage because of the marketing excellence of a retail outlet. And a pharmaceutical company may gain competitive advantage because of a discovery by a small biotech company that feeds into its development pipeline.

The converse is that competitive *disadvantages* may come from anywhere in the value chain. An auto company can lose sales because improperly designed tires hurt the safety image. A computer company can lose market share because retailers will not stock inventory. And a pharmaceutical company may lose precious time-to-market[1] because the firm conducting clinical trials is inefficient.

The evolution in management practice gives rise to the most compelling business case for supplier diversity. An investment in *developing* the suppliers in corporate value chains is an investment in their own competitive advantage. Changing demographics portend that tomorrow the majority of those value-chain partners will be diverse businesses, those owned by minorities and women.

Therefore, supplier diversity professionals have a choice: they can position themselves as a strategic asset, or they can position themselves as strategically irrelevant—for example, as avenues for corporate philanthropy, image shapers in a public relations effort, or mechanisms for compliance with mandated outsourcing quotas.

The perceived importance of the supplier diversity professionals' role—and therefore their influence over sourcing decisions—depends on the sophistication of the corporate outsourcing system. We will see that traditional *procurement* is essentially a bureaucratic process encountered in old-school corporations; value-chain *development* is a strategic imperative that drives the success of leading-edge corporations.

These different approaches to outsourcing help us understand the variety of motives underlying supplier diversity programs. Let's briefly review the various motivations to see how these shape corporations' differing approaches to supplier diversity.

MOTIVES DIFFER FOR SUPPLIER DIVERSITY PROGRAMS

Organizations have four alternative—but not exclusive—motives for seeking out diversity in their outsourcing:

- The organization's value system emphasizes diversity.
- An external mandate compels the organization to do business with diverse suppliers.
- Diverse suppliers create a competitive advantage.
- Public image can be at stake.

Let's consider each of these scenarios to understand why corporations (and, in many cases, public-sector organizations) need to have effective supplier diversity programs. Then we will look at how different the results are when the motives are pursued in a procurement-oriented versus a development-oriented outsourcing program.

1. Corporate values can drive diversity policies.

Many corporations have diversity programs because it is the right thing to do. Corporations gain a lot of benefits from operating within a social system, and some view giving back to the system as an ethical obligation. For example, IBM's commitment to diversity has been one of its corporate values dating back more than a century. To these corporations, having a workforce diversity program and a supplier diversity program is no different than having an environmental sustainability program.

The latter case is easier for some people to understand. Some corporations are "good environmental citizens," because avoiding pollution, minimizing the carbon consequences of their decisions, and giving preference to recyclable materials will result in a healthier planet. They do not mandate sustainability because of regulations, penalties, or incentives; they do it because it is consistent with their value system. The analogy is a good one because some corporations have value systems that emphasize creating opportunity and equity in society. Generating jobs in low-income communities, giving people who have been discriminated against for generations a chance to succeed, and returning the favor to disabled veterans who have made sacrifices to serve their country are ways of helping to create the kind of society they want to live in.

Other corporations have different value systems. They believe their only responsibility is to maximize shareholder wealth while obeying the letter of the law. They believe that if shareholders wish to contribute some of their dividend income to the Nature Conservancy or the NAACP (National Association for the Advancement of Colored People), then that is up to the individual shareholder; the corporation should not be making that decision for them. It is a different value system: it is what it is.

The interesting situations involve corporations that have strong workforce diversity programs and weak supplier diversity programs. That discrepancy is puzzling to outsiders, because it seems to reflect an incongruous value system, but it usually arises when the corporation has a contemporary human resource system but an antiquated outsourcing system.

2. External mandates can require supplier diversity.

Even if a corporation's values are indifferent to diversity issues, its own customers may require a diversity-friendly program. In many cases, this situation results from large corporations imposing mandates on their tier-one suppliers. The outsourcing officers of the large corporation say, in effect, "If you want to do business with us, you'd better have a supplier diversity program of your own." Some large corporations go even farther, requiring the second-tier suppliers to insist on third-tier and even fourth-tier supplier diversity programs: they are using the influence that arises from their strong purchasing power to leverage their results.

The nation's largest customer is the U.S. federal government, and its purchasing power can likewise be an instrument of social policy. The government can impose requirements that include multitier supplier diversity. In most cases, such requirements represent sound public policy, even though there will always be objectors: people who *only* consider how their self-interests are affected deride "set-aside clauses" in public-sector contracts, usually without understanding the economic wisdom of providing them.[2]

As an example of the economic wisdom of inclusion mandates, suppose a sector of society is in dire need of economic stimulus: it may be a distressed inner city, or a set of people living below the poverty line who will need public assistance if they are not enabled to become economically self-sufficient. It makes sense for the government to give them a chance to become successful business owners, so that their need for public assistance is transitory, not perpetual. This approach is more effective than providing public assistance ("welfare payments"). Recall that minority business owners hire minorities at a higher rate than do white owners, therefore, a governmental program that promotes MBE success leverages its impact through job creation: the public good outweighs the beliefs of the privileged about their entitlement.[3]

3. Diverse suppliers can create competitive advantage.

In the first half of the last century, the focus of U.S.-based corporations was on the domestic market, with white housewives being the primary consumer group for all but major purchases. In the new millennium, these corporations serve a very different market.

The women who were "in the home" in the last century are in the workplace in the new century. In fact, with the massive layoffs resulting from the recession that began in 2008, primarily resulting in job losses for men, women have been quickly approaching parity in terms of their participation in the working world. They have already broken through the old glass ceilings to penetrate the ranks of management where value-chain decisions are made. As entrepreneurs, they are operating larger and larger businesses, becoming important "B2B" customers. And because career women are often expected to "do it all," they continue to be the ones who are likely to dominate family purchase decisions. For these reasons, having an effective supplier diversity program that generates a positive image among women making outsourcing decisions at all levels creates competitive advantage.

The same analysis is applicable to racial groups. Whites are no longer the majority in most of America's largest cities, and they will lose their national majority status before mid-century. Therefore, corporations have to pay attention to *emerging domestic markets,* because these are increasingly large market segments. The suppliers and go-to-market partners who best understand their tastes, culture, outsourcing patterns, and language are minorities. Even today, major consumer goods companies or retailers cannot afford to ignore the Hispanic market (as you will recall from Figure 1.2 and Table 1.1). And, the African American market, although it is smaller and has a slower growth rate, is perhaps even more important because black-oriented culture (hip-hop is one important facet of it) has market appeal across racial groups and national boundaries. The ability to tailor offerings to emerging domestic markets by using minority businesses in key value-chain roles creates competitive advantage.

Customer loyalty is always a strategic objective, for clear economic reasons. All market research studies reach the same conclusion: it costs a lot more—at least five times more—to recruit a new customer than to retain an existing customer. So the corporation needs to be able to promote itself as being responsive to each consumer group.

The general point here is that markets are not uniform; they are highly segmented, so corporations seeking to serve these segments need to consider the economic value of cultivating a favorable public image.

Furthermore, the value chains of today's major corporations cross national boundaries. Minorities—especially immigrants or second-generation immigrants—tend to be good conduits for global distribution and global sourcing. They often have language skills, cultural knowledge, and personal or family connections that can facilitate importing and exporting. And in many countries, business deals hinge on the strength of relationships between the people committing to the deal.[4] In such circumstances, involvement of the right minority partner creates competitive advantage.

4. Public image can be at stake.

Corporate reputation matters today in a way that was not true a few decades ago, and it is much more vulnerable. Corporate policies and performance were once much more opaque, with few people paying attention. That was before the information explosion, the blogosphere, the rise of public watchdog groups, the ease of promoting significant boycotts, shareholder activism, the proliferation of media, and widespread public distrust of corporate executives.

The African American advocacy organizations were the pioneers in using publicity to reshape corporate policies to foster inclusion of minorities. But others, too, have discovered the value of public embarrassment—and, to a lesser extent, public praise—to achieve the social and economic impact that politicians have been unable or unwilling to create. As a result, there are many avenues that modern civil rights activists can take in their quest to mitigate de facto economic discrimination.

Note that a demographic group that is particularly coveted by marketers is the gay, lesbian, bisexual, and transgender (GLBT) community, a large market segment whose members tend to be affluent, educated, and closely networked. Their history of facing discrimination makes them highly attuned to which corporations are GLBT-friendly and which are not, and they communicate within the community about which corporations deserve their business and which ones are to be boycotted.

ADDING SUPPLIER DIVERSITY TO TRADITIONAL PROCUREMENT IS INEFFECTIVE

Whatever their motivation, corporations' success in achieving value-chain diversity depends on the sophistication of their outsourcing process. Adding a supplier diversity mandate to the traditional procurement approach produces dismal results, whereas a leading-edge development approach to supplier diversity actually increases the corporation's competitive advantage. Let's contrast the two approaches.

The traditional corporation can have highly refined standard operating procedures for purchasing. In the stereotypical case, it sets very specific requirements, forecasts needs, and then issues a request for information (RFI). The purchasing professionals evaluate responses to RFIs and approve a set of possible suppliers—businesses that have the capacity to bid on outsource business. Then they issue RFQs and conduct some sort of reverse auction, buying from the lowest bidder—the supplier that will meet the corporation's specified requirements at the best price.

The bidding in our example is for a one-year contract to supply an exact quantity on a predetermined delivery schedule that will fulfill 100 percent of the corporation's need for that particular outsourced item. It is an enticing piece of business for bidders because the quantity is large. So each bidder decides how thin to shave its profit margin in order to win the contract.

The winning bidder often comes to view the victory as a mixed blessing. On the plus side, the MBE has a new revenue stream and can add the customer to its "résumé" of customers the MBE has served. On the minus side, it is difficult for many diverse suppliers to scale up their operating capacity on a tight timetable to fulfill contract requirements—and avoid the penalties for lateness. And financial capacity is often stretched even farther than operating capacity, as the large corporate customer exercises its purchasing muscle by imposing extended payment terms. This can create a cash-flow crisis even without penalties for late deliveries.

Suddenly winning a large contract can create longer-term problems for the diverse business. There have been many cases in which desperate MBEs have hired workers at such a rate that the businesses were taking on "anyone with a pulse," with no time for training. To make matters worse, there were not enough supervisors to make sure the job was being done correctly—because workers could not be promoted and trained as supervisors quickly enough, and the best talent could not be taken off the production lines without hurting productivity. In such cases, the inefficiencies, delays, and quality problems drained what little profit was available from the low bid, and by the time the business was scaled up and everyone was high up on the learning curve, the contract ended and was put out for rebid.

The termination of a large contract is often more damaging than the ramp-up. Downsizing is never a simple matter of eliminating payroll costs. Layoffs are traumatic and disruptive, sapping energy and morale so that productivity typically drops below the pre-ramp-up level. During the downsizing, the best workers tend to be first to quit—even if their jobs are secure—because working in a rapidly contracting organization is unpleasant, and the best workers have the best opportunities in the outside labor market.[5] The residual workforce is of a lower quality because a lot of unsuitable people are hired during the rapid workforce buildup, when the MBE has to settle for "warm bodies" to staff the production lines or provide the services.

Worst of all, in this all-too-typical scenario, existing customers are neglected and receive low-quality, poor service as the MBE becomes preoccupied with the monumental task of fulfilling the large corporation's contract. Disgruntled existing customers give the business instead to a more responsive supplier. When this happens, the MBE's reputation is damaged among purchasing managers who "talk shop" with other purchasing managers. Worse still, those who oppose giving business to MBEs highlight the bad experience as a reason not to do business with diverse suppliers.

As a result of these dynamics, the traditional approach to purchasing can leave the diverse supplier worse off than before it secured the big corporate contract, and lucky to survive at all.

OLD-SCHOOL SUPPLIER DIVERSITY PROGRAMS HAVE INSUFFICIENT IMPACT

The major corporation in the aforementioned scenario outsourced a lot of business to minority suppliers through a process that resulted in many MBE bankruptcies. Ironically, the corporation was earning accolades for its efforts from the old-school supplier diversity establishment. That seems incomprehensible until one realizes that *what is being celebrated is compliance with the old paradigm*, not impact on the economic success of minorities.

Here is where the corporation's well-intentioned program went astray. Upon receiving the mandate to have a supplier diversity program, the corporation's Chief Purchasing Officer (CPO) found out what other old-school organizations were doing. He was told to take the following orthodox steps:

- Gain a strong mandate from top management.
- Create a high-level committee to oversee diversity-spend.
- Assign explicit responsibility to a supplier diversity program manager.
- Track diversity-spend and hold managers accountable for results.
- Show the benefits to the corporation's reputation.
- Join the prescribed advocacy/certification organizations.

Following this formula, the CPO soon found he had created a bureaucracy within a bureaucracy. The supplier diversity professionals were attending a year-round circuit of opportunity fairs and celebratory events that yielded almost no new suppliers. Meanwhile, thousands of disappointed diverse suppliers who had logged on to the corporation's Web site and visited its booth were busy blogging—criticizing the corporation for being insincere in its commitment to supplier diversity.

The problem was not lack of sincerity or commitment: the problem was inherent in trying to graft a supplier diversity program onto an outdated approach to outsourcing. Let's consider an alternative approach.

VALUE-CHAIN DEVELOPMENT IS A STRATEGIC PROCESS

The approach to outsourcing taken by leading-edge companies is strategic rather than procedural: the objective is to gain competitive advantage at the value-chain level.

Like its old-school counterpart, the leading-edge corporation also determines its requirements, forecasts its needs, and then searches out the set of possible suppliers—businesses that have the potential to help the world-class corporation succeed in the marketplace. But the next step is not to conduct a reverse auction: the next step is to rank-order the set of suppliers from best to worst, using multiple criteria, such as:

- Ability to generate business the corporation would not otherwise get
- Potential to develop as a supplier
- Low cost-structure
- High-enough quality
- Continuous improvement processes in place
- A promising research and development (R & D) pipeline
- Strong controls
- Reengineered processes
- Compatible operating strategy
- Stable capital structure
- Favorable location

- Record of success
- Diverse status

The various factors would be weighted according to the leading-edge corporation's strategic objectives and its corporate values.

But next, instead of soliciting bids, outsourcing professionals *negotiate a long-term deal* with some combination of the *best* suppliers. The supply contract is open-ended: the chosen suppliers will continue to get all of the corporation's business until they lose their competitive edge— or until the suppliers' service or product becomes technologically obsolete. The prices paid will be fairly low, because the corporation is operating in a competitive industry; nevertheless, profit margins are set high enough to keep the suppliers healthy.

Having chosen the suppliers with the highest potential to create value, the corporation actively improves its suppliers by giving them access to its own training programs, in-house experts, and consultants. The corporation is willing to share these resources because *outsource partners are substitutes for in-house operations—therefore, suppliers get treated the same way the corporation would treat its own strategic business units and its own employees.*

The leading-edge corporation is also concerned with the financial viability of its suppliers. This concern illustrates how far strategic thinking has advanced in terms of gaining competitive advantage from a superior value chain. If a supplier needs fifteen-day terms, and the leading-edge corporation has the liquidity to pay right away, then it is in the corporation's self-interest to pay early. Like its old-school counterparts, the leading-edge corporation has the purchasing power to force its suppliers to accept terms that increase its own bottom line in the short run. But it is ultimately self-defeating to exploit suppliers: they need money to invest in infrastructure, R & D, and process improvements, all of which benefit the corporation in the long run. That is why payment terms are negotiated: the objective is to achieve maximum strategic benefit, not to extract every last dollar out of the contract terms.

The leading-edge corporation would also consider making an equity investment in its high-potential suppliers. The corporation's motive is twofold:

- The corporation gains control by having its own representatives on the boards of important suppliers. This reduces the risk that they will make bad strategic or operating decisions that will threaten their survival and, consequently, the integrity of the value chain and the corporation's competitive advantage.

- Injecting equity funding improves the capital structure of its important suppliers, lowering their cost of capital (thus enabling them to offer the corporation better pricing) and raising their borrowing capacity—which might be helpful should the corporation experience an upsurge in demand.

Obviously, leading-edge corporations approach outsourcing from a very different perspective than their old-school counterparts. Suppliers are seen as value-chain partners that can contribute to competitive advantage, and they are treated as such.

A DEVELOPMENTAL APPROACH BENEFITS SUPPLIER DIVERSITY

The evolution of the purchasing paradigm toward supply chain management requires a parallel evolution of the supplier diversity paradigm. Both need to be strategically focused, and both need to move beyond the simplistic old-school dictum of maximizing shareholder wealth.

The old-school approach focused on a single bottom line:[6] short-term profitability. But leading-edge corporations have a more sophisticated concept of what it means to be doing well as a corporation. Their achievements are judged in terms of "the triple bottom line," which takes into account social and ecological performance, as well as financial performance.[7]

Guided by this broader perspective, the outsourcing approach of the leading-edge corporation is more strategic than procedural. The focus is on long-term competitive advantage at the value-chain level, in the context of good corporate citizenship. Many corporations *say* they have strong values, as you can see in any glossy annual report or read on any corporate Web site, but the leading-edge corporation actually *lives up* to them.

DIVERSITY STRATEGY IS A FACET OF OUTSOURCING STRATEGY

The role of corporations in an economic system is to create value for customers, which entitles the corporations to receive a revenue stream as a reward for their contributions. But they do not do all of the value-creation work in-house. They assess their own core competencies, capacity, and profit opportunities, and then they make a strategic decision about what work is to be done in-house and what is to be done through outsourcing.

The outsourced work is performed by three sets of businesses:

1. Value-added suppliers occupy direct value-chain roles. They are the corporation's tiers of suppliers upstream in the value chain and the go-to-market partners in the downstream distribution channel.

2. Support suppliers enable the corporation to operate its key business processes. They do not add direct value to the product or service but are indispensible in keeping operations running. They include suppliers of such functions as repairs, utilities, maintenance and overhaul, transportation, and various essential services. The term "industry cluster" refers to the set of support suppliers essential to the functioning of major industries.[8]

3. Peripheral suppliers have no direct value-chain roles: that is, how well they perform has no impact on the core business. Landscaping, refuse hauling, promotional products, generic supplies, and most temporary staffing services fall into this category: it does not make much difference to the corporation that provides these goods and services—and, in many cases, if nobody does.

Old-school corporations tend to confine their diverse outsourcing to peripheral suppliers, even while achieving a large diversity-spend. That is, if one looks beyond the raw number of dollars spent with diverse firms, one usually sees a preponderance of nonessential goods and services being bought, usually at low profit margins. Purchasing agents sometimes refer to these as "commodity items," signifying that the suppliers are undifferentiated: the corporation is no better off or worse off if the supplier is excellent, bad, or mediocre. The corporate accounts payable to diverse firms gets recorded, the recognition awards get accepted and publicized, and the mainstream business community continues to look very white and very masculine.

The leading-edge corporation's executives have a different vision of what is possible: they see a future in which the demographics of their value chain will match the demographics of the society in which it operates. They aspire to create real inclusion, not just to comply with mandates that token involvement will satisfy. They actually believe that the American Dream should be a reality: if you have the talent, persistence, work ethic, and ingenuity, you ought to be able to succeed no matter what your gender, race, ethnicity, sexual orientation, or veteran status. They recognize that business has not been a level playing field in their lifetimes, and that some fledgling businesses will need to be helped, up to the point where they must prove themselves. The ones that succeed will become valuable and loyal business allies.

As we noted earlier, outsourcing that follows old-school procurement practices was simple: issue the specifications and give the business to the supplier with the lowest price—or, when there is a supplier diversity constraint, to the diverse supplier with the lowest price.

Outsourcing at the leading-edge corporation is complex, because decisions are made in the context of a strategic, long-term perspective that considers multiple factors. One important consideration is geographic proximity. A general rule is that developing local suppliers is preferable to sourcing from low-cost countries (contrary to the most recent management fad that has driven herds of corporate buyers to China and India). The leading-edge corporation rank orders its supplier location preferences as follows: within the home community, within the state, within the region, within the country, and then wherever global best value can be obtained.

The following factors drive leading-edge thinking about supplier location:

1. It is in the corporation's self-interest to sustain a healthy local economy.

    The highest net revenue opportunities today are in the knowledge economy, with the service economy coming in at a close second, and the manufacturing and agricultural economies coming in some distance behind. Success in the knowledge and service economies depends on the quality of the workforce—on the human capital of the corporation. As many of the Midwest's cities have found out, it is hard to attract the best talent to work in distressed urban environments. Placement professionals get a response that takes the form of, "It sounds like a great job, but who would want to live there? Furthermore, I have a family to raise; I'm not sure I want them growing up in that environment." The problem extends beyond attracting the nation's best professional talent: if the city is economically distressed, then the local workforce is likely to have a low literacy level, because educational attainment is largely determined by the wealth being created in the local community.

The more corporations buy locally, the greater the wealth that gets created—and then recirculated—in the local economy. That creates local jobs, which results in decreased "welfare" costs and increased tax revenues. The city, therefore, has more money to invest in the school system, to maintain and improve the infrastructure, to lure industry clusters, and to otherwise make the city an attractive place for key employees to live and to operate the business. The value of the corporation's real estate also increases, and its insurance costs go down as the crime rate subsides.

2. The real costs of outsourcing favor businesses that are closer rather than farther away.

Accountants are quick to point out that life-cycle costs are more important to decision makers than simple acquisition costs. This means that a low invoice price may not represent high value when total costs are calculated. Yet the latter metric is overlooked when old-school purchasing agents' performance is appraised on the basis of invoice price.

As we accumulate experience in purchasing from low-cost countries, we are learning that prudent corporations will add in a cost that would monetize the increased risk. Many corporations have rejoiced in achieving large apparent savings only to discover quality deficiencies, contaminants (sometimes deadly ones), and delivery delays that can bring operations to a halt. Increasingly, corporate executives are coming to realize that lower costs of offshoring tactics do not necessarily result in better outsourcing decisions.

Furthermore, total cost, in the new era, is not just measured in monetary terms. There are also societal costs to be considered by any organization that takes into account corporate social responsibility, whether or not these can be translated into dollar consequences. The most urgent of these costs relates to the carbon consequences of outsourcing decisions. Thus, for example, if components can be manufactured locally, then the corporation does not cause raw materials to be shipped halfway around the world to be processed at low wage rates (and with lax pollution controls), and then the manufactured components to be shipped halfway around the world back to the corporation. This practice may reduce the purchase price of components in dollar terms, but it increases greenhouse gas emissions as a result of consuming enormous quantities of nonrenewable fossil fuels. It is increasingly difficult to argue that this practice results in greater value for the customer or the shareholder, both of whose environment is being harmed by such outsourcing decisions.

3. Proximity tends to maximize flexibility and time-based competitive advantage.

Some businesses have highly predictable, steady demand that permits long outsourcing lead times. Examples might include Christmas cards, structural steel for bridges, road salt, beer, and education. Other businesses can have sudden changes in demand, such as hospitals, manufacturers of bomb detectors, convention centers, flexible manufacturing with a just-in-time system, the music industry, and most high-technology businesses. When flexibility is important, the closer the supplier, the greater the corporation's competitive advantage.

This is generally the case, because on short notice the corporation can get local suppliers to reshuffle production batches, make emergency deliveries, open up a second shift, or run down their inventory safety stock and provide the increase in supply. Such responsiveness is infeasible when purchasing from low-cost countries. Even if the supplier can get a container load of the components to the dock in China that same day, the container ship needs to make the transit, get unloaded, and then the container needs to get through customs, get reloaded onto a truck, and then delivered to the receiving dock weeks or months later.

Of course, there are supply situations where distance makes no difference to competitive advantage—such as in the case of some call centers, some X-ray interpretation, and some software writing—because delivery is at the speed of electricity. But these are exceptions to a general rule that has a lot of validity.

4. Outsourcing always involves problems, and problems are more difficult to solve the farther away your supplier is.

There are always issues to resolve with suppliers: clarifying communications, correcting quality problems, adjusting requirements, improving cross-organizational processes, or resolving disputes. That is why there is a need for outsourcing professionals: they cannot be replaced by electronic-order placers—corporate outsourcing is not at all like ordering a book over the Internet.

If the supplier is local, then it can be visited or called in to meet with the affected corporate departments. If the supplier is somewhere in Asia, then those convenient and highly effective problem-solving options are not available—even if there are no language barriers.

5. The corporation needs to be careful about creating competitors.

Major corporations take on major roles in value chains; they outsource minor roles to suppliers. The better those suppliers understand how the corporation creates value, the more effective they can be in supporting the corporation as a supplier. But this knowledge also makes them better prepared to take over the corporation's role in the value chain.

Imagine you are a foreign corporation or an economic development official in that country looking for opportunities to expand business. One option is to start from scratch, do the research and development work, and set up an indigenous industry. An easier way is to see where myopic old-school corporations are making R & D and market-development investments, offer to become a key supplier on very generous terms, learn all about the business, and then set up a competing operation in your own low-wage region.

The business relationships created by the corporation's outsourcing system make it more or less likely that a supplier would take over the corporation's role in the value chain. In the traditional procurement paradigm, there are no expectations, no loyalties, no obligations, and no vestiges of goodwill once the contract terms have been completed. In fact, the heavy-handed traditional corporation will be lucky if its suppliers are not harboring resentment over the way they were treated and, as a result, thirsting for revenge.

In contrast, the leading-edge corporation's emphasis on *development of* suppliers—rather than on *procurement from* suppliers—would create a relationship that would minimize the danger of waking up one day to find that your supplier is now your competitor. And local disadvantaged suppliers would be the most loyal, because they would be getting the most help, as a result of being the most needy.

6. Intellectual property becomes very difficult to protect the farther away the outsourcing organization is.

The United States has a legal system that discourages theft of intellectual property, and it provides mechanisms for seeking remedies if intellectual property is violated. Most countries to which large corporations can outsource have appropriate laws on the books, but it can be very difficult to get the laws enforced against one of their own supplier companies. Of course, the risk depends on the country involved: for example, Singapore has the reputation of being a safe place to do business, but China has the opposite reputation.

The more important the supplier's role in the corporate value chain, the greater the access to the corporation's intellectual property. Thus corporations are better off outsourcing to domestic suppliers if there is significant danger that intellectual property can be misappropriated.

7. The regulatory environment matters more the farther away your supplier is.

   Outsourcing involves giving up some of the control that a vertically integrated organization exercises by doing everything in-house. In the case of a domestic supplier, the purchasing agent can make some assumptions about what can be expected. These expectations are encoded in such treatises as the Uniform Commercial Code, the Food and Drug Administration Regulations, the body of case law that governs commerce, and the laws of the state in which the corporation writes contracts. The problem with offshore sourcing is that these regulatory mechanisms do not readily extend beyond U.S. borders. That means the purchasing department, exercising due diligence, needs to verify many things that can be assumed if working with a U.S. supplier, especially a local supplier bound by common state law.

8. Dependence on a supplier can be a significant risk where there is political instability.

   Most of the major industrialized countries have strong, stable governments. That stability minimizes the risk of nasty surprises that can threaten the continuity of supply. But most of these countries have high labor costs and strong regulatory mechanisms. In contrast, many low-cost countries have fragile political institutions and corrupt regulatory mechanisms, and cost savings are partly due to lax enforcement of anti-pollution, worker-safety, and even child-labor laws. In the long run, these regimes are unstable, and, as a result, so are the business arrangements that seem to be such a good deal. Lower cost ends up once again being correlated with higher risk.

The leading-edge corporation's executives take into account the aforementioned eight factors when making outsourcing decisions. They conclude that *it is generally preferable to develop domestic suppliers with strong loyalty ties to the corporation.* When this rule of thumb gets applied in the context of pursuing a triple bottom line, the business case for supplier diversity becomes compelling.

The leading-edge corporation aspires to be a formidable competitor, operating within a strong and healthy community. To achieve the latter, it needs to develop minorities and women as excellent value-chain partners so that they can contribute fully to the corporation's success as well as to the local economy. Diverse suppliers need to supply the corporation, but they also need to create jobs, local wealth, role models, and career paths for local citizens. That will make the community more attractive to the technical and management professionals the corporation needs to recruit from the nationwide pool. The spending and re-spending in the local economy will fund improvements in the area's school systems that prepare the local workforce to work at the corporation. The approach is strategic and based on corporate long-term self-interest.

In practice, the leading-edge corporation looks locally first, and then it broadens the search for suppliers until the corporation achieves the degree of value-chain diversity it seeks. It does not approach the recruitment task passively, by attending the opportunity fairs at the national conventions and collecting business cards. Nor does it issue RFQs to which diverse businesses are urged to respond; the corporation is much more proactive. Its supplier diversity professionals are talent scouts. Their job is very different from their counterparts at old-school companies, who often feel like orphans begging for favors at the door of the purchasing department.

The leading-edge corporation starts by making a strategic decision about which value-chain activities to retain and which ones to outsource. The decision is based on the corporation's core competency, need for control, cost of capital, internal capacity, and other strategic considerations, and it can involve value-added suppliers, support suppliers, or peripheral suppliers. Then criteria for success are established so that outsourcing professionals will know how well they are performing. Buying locally and doing business with diverse suppliers will be among the criteria for successful outsourcing.

When the need has been specified, outsourcing professionals identify candidates that can provide the necessary goods and services. This is where the development-oriented approach creates impact *and* competitive advantage.

The corporation can insist that a key majority supplier help develop the best diverse supplier, resulting in an effective mentor-protégé program. Not only does the corporation encourage its best suppliers to bring along diverse partners that can be improved, but the corporation puts all of its corporate resources behind the continuous improvement process, as we discussed earlier. It provides favorable payment terms if the diverse supplier has cash-flow constraints, and perhaps even provides some equity. It helps the diverse business acquire some form of board-level oversight. It opens up its training programs to everyone in the supply chain, and it assigns in-house experts and consultants to help them become what they are capable of becoming.

Suppose, though, that the corporation has decided to outsource goods and services that it has been providing internally, but that there are no diverse suppliers in that particular business. All is not lost, because the corporation's outsourcing professionals are talent scouts, remember? The corporation might, for example, decide to spin off to a minority owner the division it no longer wants to support. The talent scouts will first look for a minority or woman within the division who is capable of running it as a freestanding operation. If there is no qualified insider, then the talent scouts will look for a suitable outsider who can become the new owner/operator. The transitional ownership and funding issues need to be carefully thought out, because it would be unethical to create "a front company"—one that *seemed* to be minority- or woman-owned and operated but, in fact, was not. But those are challenges, not showstoppers, to experts who understand leveraged buyouts, earn-outs, the various venture capital options, and loan arrangements. Once the new company is stood up, it can be partnered with another supplier so that the corporation will not be overly dependent on a unitary source of supply (earthquakes, fires, and bankruptcies *do* happen!).

The leading-edge corporation in our example demonstrates what is possible if corporations take a development approach rather than adding a supplier diversity function to a traditional procurement operation. The former involves a commitment to making it happen; the latter involves going through the motions and hoping for the best. Both require considerable effort: the old-school approach has little chance of succeeding; the leading-edge approach strengthens the entire value chain.

It should be an easy choice, but accomplishing the transition calls for a paradigm shift, and there will naturally be resistance. The resistance will most likely come from everyone who has a vested interest in the old way of doing things—from purchasing agents, to supplier diversity professionals, to the government agencies and advocacy organizations that can institutionalize the status quo.

Meanwhile, minorities currently make up 30 percent of the population, but they own only 15 percent of the businesses, and they bring in only 3 percent of the business revenues.[9] We have a system that is not helping minorities very much.

We can do a lot better.

CONCLUDING THOUGHTS

Corporate supplier diversity programs consume a lot of money and time, but they have not yielded the level of impact that one would require of any other effort that had been going on for more than a quarter of a century. There are very few large-scale minority- or women-owned businesses. And their contribution to the U.S. economy is far below their proportions in the U.S. population.

Even some of the corporate programs with high diversity-spend do not look so impressive when we examine what is being outsourced. If diverse firms are relegated to supplying goods and services that do not really matter, then these businesses are not being helped to become full participants in the mainstream economy. They are simply being given peripheral roles in value chains. Token involvement falls short of the meaningful inclusion that supplier diversity programs are intended to facilitate.

The existing supplier diversity paradigm is not working. Yet the supplier diversity establishment accepts the traditional procurement approach to outsourcing as a "given" and urges corporations to graft a supplier development mandate onto it. When urging has not worked, we have tried to impose the mandate onto the procurement process by stern instructions from the CEO, by forming committees with oversight responsibility, and by creating systems to catch and punish noncompliance with the directives. These more forceful approaches have not made much of a difference either.

The required paradigm shift—*from procurement to development*—is not only good for minorities and women seeking meaningful value-chain participation, but it is good for corporations: it increases competitive advantage. And by so doing, it enables supplier diversity professionals to articulate a compelling business case for why the entire management structure needs to be supporting supplier diversity initiatives.

5 SUPPORT ORGANIZATIONS SHOULD REFOCUS ON CORE MISSION

EXECUTIVE SUMMARY

Many support organizations have the mission to foster diverse suppliers' participation in the U.S. economy. They may have such names as councils, centers, chambers of commerce, associations, round tables, leagues, caucuses, congresses, or alliances. And they range from small part-time offices to national-scope organizations with many satellites. Each support organization has a specific niche, with its own constituency, set of activities, and population subgroup.

Collectively, support organizations have taken us beyond where we were when the Civil Rights Act banned discrimination. But they have not created the impact that is needed to achieve diverse participation in mainstream value chains at the level of parity. Nor are they currently positioned to change outcomes significantly from what we see today. They need to refocus on their core mission, which is to create a different future for the demographic group they are intended to serve.

The support organizations all advocate giving business to their particular constituents. The range of services offered includes certification, access to contracts, access to capital, consulting, education, assistance in planning community economic development, matchmaking, shaping public policy, and celebratory events. But no support organization has chosen to perform all of the needed roles, and most diverse enterprises receive none of these services.

The support functions that will have the most impact are advocacy, certification, capacity development, and matchmaking, in that order. Most other activities are of secondary importance and, often, a strategic distraction—hence the need for strategic refocusing.

Advocacy involves making the business case to corporations and shaping public policy to achieve diverse inclusion in mainstream value chains.

Certification must be conducted to rigorous standards to prevent fraud, but at the same time it needs to be focused on the needs of diverse business enterprises (DBEs) and organizations that want to do business with them. Support organizations should certify eligibility for inclusion in *all* of the relevant diverse categories, ascertaining whether a business is owned and operated by minorities, women, veterans, and/or service-disabled veterans, and located in a particular city, county, state, and HUB Zone. The burden should never fall on DBEs to go through certification more than once: if it happens, the support organizations have failed them.

Capacity development is important. To fulfill a sustainable role in a value chain, the DBEs must deliver real value; otherwise, support organizations are accomplishing little more than channeling corporate philanthropy in the form of diversity-spend. Development of capacity involves ensuring that DBEs have adequate access to education, mentoring, technical consulting, capital, and whatever other assistance is needed to enable their success.

Matchmaking provides access to outsourcing networks that have historically excluded diverse businesses. Purchasing managers tend to stick with suppliers who have been reliable and easy to deal with, particularly when alternative suppliers add little incremental value; matchmaking arranges conversations that otherwise would be unlikely to take place. But the opportunity forums that have been a tradition among support organizations are expensive and inefficient, producing low yields for both buyers and sellers; in most cases, they result in token diversity-spend with little longer-term impact on diverse businesses and distressed communities. The matchmaking process needs to be reengineered.

Support organizations must refocus on the *impact* they are achieving. The limited accomplishments to date are partly attributable to low priority being given to supplier diversity by most corporations, public-sector agencies, and political entities; this situation calls for stronger advocacy. But the low impact is also partly attributable to the shortcomings of the various support organizations. Too often, certification reflects the organization's claimed territory rather than the DBE's needs, advocacy focuses on encouraging DBE inclusion in bidding rather than ensuring DBE development, disproportionate resources are allocated to ritualistic events, decentralized field operations are understaffed and underfunded, and the emphasis is on activities and publicity when it needs to be on creating significant impact.

Thus support organizations need to step back and ask the hard questions about whether they are fulfilling their core mission of reversing economic underparticipation. Their challenge is large and complex, calling for concerted action and a multifaceted solution. This requires visionary, collaborative leadership and a willingness to move beyond the traditions that were established in the 1980s. The business world has changed a lot since then, and the need for minority inclusion has increased dramatically.

SUPPORT ORGANIZATIONS SHOULD REFOCUS ON CORE MISSION

Prior to the 1960s and 1970s, America had a social system in place that favored white Anglo-Saxon Protestant men and actively discriminated against minorities, women, Native Americans, other religions, and people from certain countries of origin. The Civil Rights Act made discrimination illegal, and the Executive Order that established affirmative action forced organizations to redress historical inequities.

These developments were not end points in the nation's quest to live up to its value system; they were simply turning points that put the nation on the path toward social change. We were to discover that laws can be changed quickly, but cultural change is slow—it involves a nationwide change in attitudes, habits, working relationships, textbooks, norms, vocabularies, stereotypes, assumptions about societal roles, and the composition of power elites.

It was *the system* that had been responsible for the social discrimination, and the system was deeply embedded in American culture. That is why it has taken the passing of a generation of people steeped in the old traditions to render racism, sexism, and expression of various forms of hatred socially unacceptable[1] today.

Social discrimination has largely ended, at least in its overt forms. What has persisted has been economic discrimination, a system that has resulted in the net assets of minorities being an order of magnitude lower than that of their white majority counterparts. Not coincidentally, their rates of unemployment, incarceration, substance abuse, school dropout, and family disintegration are much higher. As we noted earlier, this is not just "their" problem. Their economic underperformance is at best a lost opportunity to bolster gross domestic product; at worst, it is a drain of public resources as communities allocate scarce resources to welfare, policing, prisons, and rehabilitation. Those resources would be better invested in infrastructure, health care, research and development, education, attracting or establishing the necessary industry clusters, homeland security, and defense.

Economic discrimination is also the result of *the system*. But in the domain of commerce, it is the business system rather than the national culture that causes the exclusion. And it is the biased business system that creates the need for a highly effective, impact-focused network of support organizations.

Support organizations have a core mission to make the system work for diverse businesses. They need to be held accountable for achieving results. What gets measured gets done, so their key performance indicators need to reflect their mission. Thus support organizations should be judged on their overall impact in achieving diverse participation in mainstream value chains.

Of course, any managers being judged will be tempted to choose metrics that they can easily achieve, even if these are tangential to the core mission. In the case of DBE support organizations, metrics such as the number of DBEs certified, the number of corporations providing support money, attendance at conventions, and diversity-spend all have the potential to mislead us into believing that real progress is being made when diverse businesses in fact are not much better off. For example, many DBEs get no business at all after being certified; many of the corporations that give money to the support organizations and attend their conventions have dismal records of supplier diversity; and, diversity-spend can be confined to low-profit, low-growth-potential commodity items.

If the real goal is to achieve diverse inclusion in major value chains, then focusing on helping DBEs to become a peripheral supplier, whose goods or services are "commodities," does not accomplish the mission. As we noted in Chapter 4, real inclusion has been achieved when diverse businesses become strategic partners playing important roles in value chains. Those roles create sustainable revenue streams, which are elusive when diverse involvement is limited to dispensable roles with low profitability and uncertain revenue streams.

The nation needs its support organizations to be effective in reversing the effects of centuries of economic discrimination. As we saw in Chapter 2, it is in the national interest—as well as in the interests of corporations and public-sector agencies—that diverse businesses succeed, create local wealth, and demonstrate that entrepreneurship is a realistic option for people who have the drive and talent to run their own businesses.

We must recognize that while the core mission of support organizations is to make the system work for diverse businesses, *a secondary priority* is to help the outsourcing managers in public- and private-sector organizations operate successful supplier diversity programs. The outsourcing decision makers need to ascertain the following:

- that these are, indeed, the diverse businesses they purport to be;
- that there is a match between what they want to outsource and what the diverse supplier can provide;
- that the diverse supplier be adequately financed, both in terms of capital structure (the amount of debt relative to equity) and working capital (the ability to finance ongoing cash-flow needs); and,
- that the diverse supplier is or becomes as good as it can be, because value-chain strength determines the outsourcer's competitive advantage (in the case of the private sector) and organizational effectiveness (in the case of the public sector).

Support organizations could be helpful to outsourcing managers in all of the aforementioned areas, but most of them have chosen a narrower role. Some advocate for women-owned business enterprises (WBEs), irrespective of race, while others advocate for race, irrespective of gender; some serve DBE interests, while others serve corporate interests; some serve specific ethnic groups, while others serve all ethnic groups; some deal only with private-sector inclusion, while others deal only with the public sector; some provide certification, while others do not; and some develop diverse businesses, while others take no responsibility for improving their diverse suppliers' capacity to perform.

No support organization provides a full spectrum of support services. And, collectively, the support organizations are not meeting the needs of the diverse business population: this is a problem, because *the number of diverse businesses is expanding faster than the coverage is being offered by the nation's support organizations.*

KEY PERFORMANCE INDICATORS SHOULD REFLECT THE CORE MISSION

It is worth repeating that the core mission of any support organization is to ensure the inclusion of diverse businesses in the economy. This is true whether the support organization helps corporations or public-sector agencies find good value-chain partners, advocates that such entities do business with diverse companies, or represents a particular group of minorities, women, or Native Americans. It is also worth repeating the general principle that what gets measured gets done.

Key performance indicators are metrics used to measure whether the organization is accomplishing its core mission. They keep leaders focused on the overall goal and are used by boards to hold executives accountable for results.

The ultimate criteria of support organization effectiveness is how many diverse businesses are being drawn into mainstream value chains, how many jobs are being created in economically distressed communities, or how much incremental wealth is being created by minorities, women, or Native Americans. Anything else is a secondary mission objective. It is fair for boards to ask leaders if they are making a difference. It is irresponsible to accept as a response how many clients are paying dues, how many people attend events, or how much publicity is being generated.

A secondary objective of support organizations is to remain economically viable so that they can carry out their mission. Because these are nonprofit organizations, they do not have to make a return on investment; but they do need to generate and sustain enough of a revenue stream to do their work. Most of them also need to grow to scale: a huge number of diverse businesses need to be served, and while rationing services is a short-term solution, expanding scale is necessary because the population being served is rapidly increasing.

Another important secondary objective is cost-effectiveness. All resources—from budgets to staff time—are limited, so it matters how the allocations are prioritized. The crucial question in any decision is whether a different allocation would have left diverse businesses better off. Suppose, for example, an organization purports to develop a particular group of suppliers, but a large percentage of the budget and the effort and attention of the staff goes into large-scale celebratory events. Some organizational scholars contend that an organization's real strategy can be inferred from the choices it makes, not from what is stated on the Web site or in the annual report. From this perspective, the organization in our example is really in the business of staging the large events, not developing suppliers.

Or look at fund-raising. This can take on a life of its own in nonprofits, and it has become such a problem that charitable organizations get audited to ascertain what percentage of donations actually go to the program that donors wish to support. A support organization certainly needs to be oriented toward fund-raising, because this is what allows the organization to get its work done for the DBEs. But the organization has gone too far when the operating strategy is to do whatever is necessary to raise the money—and then to be so busy raising money that the organization never gets around to ensuring that DBEs achieve their full potential to create value for their customers.

Sociologists have documented the tendency of all organizations to start out being focused on mission and then to gradually shift the focus toward self-perpetuation.[2] The antidotes are mission clarity, measurement of key performance indicators, board-level accountability, and leadership succession.

DILUTION OF EFFORT IMPAIRS MISSION ACCOMPLISHMENT

All of the support organizations have less scale and less funding than they need to accomplish their mission. For example, there are over 4 million minority-owned businesses in the United States, but only a fraction of these businesses is being served. The coverage is even worse for the nation's women-owned businesses.[3] And the farther one gets from major metropolitan areas, the sparser the support.

In this context, it is surprising that some "national" support organizations are diverting some of their resources—time and attention, particularly—to setting up supplier diversity programs in other countries, even while they are underserving their national core constituency.

Economists advocate calculating the opportunity costs of any course of action: this involves assessing *what else* the organization could be doing with the resources being allocated to a particular activity. Strategists echo that perspective, adding in the dictum that it is important to focus on the core mission and achieve those objectives before devoting "slack" resources to secondary objectives. Decision theorists caution us to beware of the distracting effect of rationalization, whereby smart people making unwise decisions[4] are able to provide explanations—to themselves as well as to others—that justify a course of action they chose.

Dilution of effort occurs when the core mission remains unfulfilled and scarce resources are allocated to a lower-priority activity. Consider the board's responsibility in the following hypothetical example:

A major U.S.-based corporation is a large donor to the support organization and has board representation. This corporation is focused on generating diversity-spend numbers and wants to count diverse suppliers from outside the United States. Its head of supplier diversity urges the national support organization to clone itself in another country. The support organization, although already spread too thin, complies, allocating scarce time and attention to a locale outside of its strategic domain. Someone on the board questions whether this is a strategic opportunity or a strategic distraction in the context of the support organization's core mission.

This scenario is likely to give rise to a lively debate, because there are no right answers. But there are honest answers. And there are also answers that rationalize one's own actions. Wisdom involves knowing which is which.

PRESENTING THE BUSINESS CASE IS KEY TO SUCCESSFUL ADVOCACY

Advocates hope to influence executive decisions and organizational processes. But decision makers and policy shapers can choose whether or not they want to be influenced. Corporations have a spectrum of motives for complying or resisting appeals for greater diverse inclusion in their value chains. The motives span the range from guilt to economic self-interest to fear of consumer boycotts.

Moral suasion is the purest form of advocacy, but it is often the least powerful. It involves explaining what a good citizen should do. It elicits philanthropic motivation. But the outsourcing departments—not the corporate philanthropy departments—decide whether a diverse supplier will get any business. The purchasing agents' motive to avoid feelings of guilt can be easily overshadowed by being held accountable for bottom-line savings and reliable delivery. Those motives favor giving repeat business to existing majority suppliers.

Appealing to economic self-interest is a much more powerful approach, but support organizations have not generally done a good job of presenting the business case. The basic logic is easy to explain to decision makers:

- Corporations should do business with diverse providers because with changing demographics these businesses must become an increasingly large component of their value chains—and therefore an increasingly important determinant of corporate competitive advantage. Furthermore, diverse providers are likely to help corporations adapt and appeal to emerging domestic markets, and to help arrange and manage cross-border importing or exporting business in countries where diverse providers can facilitate trade relationships.[5]

• Government agencies should do business with diverse suppliers for additional reasons. As minority- and women-owned businesses grow as a percentage of the entrepreneurial economy, their success will determine the vitality of the U.S. economy and national competitive advantage. Their success also plays a key role in implementing an urban strategy because minority businesses hire a larger percentage of minorities, and they create vibrant local economies, jobs, career paths, and positive role models for young people in distressed inner cities. Or, put more crudely, in the long run it is more cost-effective for governments to give disadvantaged businesses some contracts than to pay for welfare and other social programs.

Advocacy that involves threats is the most powerful persuasive message. The central argument is that the corporation will want to avoid reprisals if business is denied to diverse suppliers. Reprisals can take the form of loss of contract volume, lawsuits, or boycotts. Laws, executive orders, and policy directives can all carry threats that discourage noncompliance with a supplier diversity initiative. Advocacy groups can harm a corporation's reputation by publicizing noncooperation, and, today, the Internet is a powerful tool for making the threat real. And sympathetic politicians can be persuaded to put pressure on corporations that directly or indirectly do business with the government.

Threats should be a last resort after other advocacy approaches have failed. The motivation to avoid reprisals is the least desirable because it creates resistance and backlash: people resent being forced to do things. But if threat tactics are used, they must be used well. If a threat proves hollow, then the advocate has little subsequent credibility.

THE MOST EFFECTIVE SUPPORT INCLUDES SUPPLIER DEVELOPMENT

Whichever advocacy approach is used to create opportunities, diverse businesses need to be *developed* so they can achieve their potential. Yet few support organizations do much to develop their DBEs.

Here is where leadership vision and collaboration between support organizations can significantly increase impact. One organization may be very effective at advocating—shaping public policy, gaining a top management mandate, or modifying procurement processes—but not good at preparing diverse providers to take on the business; other support organizations may be much better at developing DBE capacity. They obviously ought to get together and leverage each other's strengths.

Said another way, advocacy will not achieve strong results without developing the businesses being championed. Enabling DBE success involves several activities. DBEs will need access to contracts which, in practical terms, means that a channel will have to be provided that matches diverse suppliers with opportunities. Then, DBEs will in most cases need access to capital: new contracts at least require working capital, but DBEs may also need to lay out cash to scale up to perform on the contract—to expand floor space, acquire capital equipment, or hire additional employees. And the entrepreneurs will need to acquire the knowledge to use the capital wisely and perform on the contract in a way that generates repeat or referral business. Helping to increase DBE business acumen may take the form of management and technical assistance or intensive learning experiences, that is, consulting or education. Consulting addresses immediate challenges; education provides longer-term benefits.

CERTIFICATION SHOULD HELP—NOT BURDEN—DBES

Certification is a good thing: it prevents people from creating "front companies"—companies that masquerade as MBEs or WBEs but are really owned and run by majority corporations or husbands. The certification process is a form of auditing. It is necessary because people who lack ethics will misrepresent ownership and control to secure business that would not rightfully come to them—business that is being reserved for diverse enterprises.

The quality and value of certification spans the range from self-certification to over-certification. Self-certification is no certification at all. High-quality certification generates confidence that the business is primarily owned and managed by people who fit the diverse category. Redundant certification places an unnecessary burden on the diverse company.

Certification needs to be construed as a service to DBEs and the out-sourcing managers who give them business. It should never be a money maker for support organizations. *The core mission of support organizations*[6] is to support DBEs, not to tax them and hamper them with redundant paperwork. The goal of corporate and public-sector supplier diversity programs is to foster the success of diverse value-chain providers which, in the case of obtaining required certification, means sheltering the DBEs from red tape that adds no further value. Corporations want diverse suppliers to concentrate their efforts on creating value, driving out costs, and engaging in continuous improvement—not spending unnecessary hours obtaining multiple certifications. So here is the general rule: There is *never* justification for a diverse business to have undergone more than one high-quality certification.

This does not mean that support organizations should certify that a business falls into a generic category of being a "diverse business enterprise." That would be a mistake, because public policy and corporate policy will at times need to target for inclusion particular groups, such as women, minorities, veterans, Native Americans, businesses located in HUB Zones, and so on. What it does mean is that if a woman minority entrepreneur has gone through the high-quality NMSDC certification to establish that the business is, indeed, owned and operated by a minority, then the audit should also certify that the business is woman owned. Conversely, if a woman entrepreneur has gone though the equally high-quality Women's Business Enterprise National Council (WBENC) certification to establish that the business is, indeed, owned and operated by a woman who also is a minority, then the audit should also certify that the business is minority owned.[7] At the same time, both organizations should be able to inspect military papers and ascertain whether the business could also be certified as veteran owned.

Certifying authorities have in some cases been criticized for being territorial, bureaucratic, self-serving, arrogant, and slow. When that criticism is valid, certification is an impediment to minority success rather than a facilitator of minority engagement. A diverse supplier that fits many categories—for example, MBE, WBE, SDV, HUB Zone, city resident, state resident—may be required to obtain multiple certifications. The duplicative processes require an unnecessary commitment of DBE time and long delays, when a single thorough assessment is all that is needed.

Certification should be standardized, just like audits, electrical outlets, pilot's licenses, and ATMs. A common high-quality certification process can be used by every certifying agency; some of the paperwork processing could be centralized to increase efficiency and uniform quality; and certifications should be accepted by all public- and private-sector buyers.

Until we create national certification, the rule should be, simply, that the *certification conducted to the higher standard must always be accepted by someone who would settle for a lower standard.*

MOST LARGE MATCHMAKING EVENTS NEED REENGINEERING

Traditional matchmaking happens at "opportunity fairs," where a large number of DBEs will make the rounds to visit a set of corporate and public-sector booths. This is an expensive way to bring together buyers and sellers, and it is largely ineffective, as evidenced by the very low yield to buyers and the degree of frustration and cynicism expressed by DBEs.

Why does this format not work? It does not work because, in practice, almost all of the DBEs the supplier diversity professional encounters in this forum lack the capacity to meet the needs of their organizations. These corporations (or public-sector organizations) have a finite number of specific outsourcing opportunities. The opportunities either involve commodities (such as staffing, IT, janitorial supplies, premiums, office supplies, safety products, etc.) or industry-specific strategic outsourcing. If the buyer is interested in commodities, then these can be procured by an RFI (request for information about business capacity) to qualify eligible bidders, followed by a reverse auction, without need for any interaction at an opportunity fair. If the buyer is interested in strategic outsourcing, then traditional opportunity fairs are an inefficient and largely impractical means of seeking out qualified vendors.

The buyer would have a much higher probability of establishing a supply relationship by participating in an industry-specific forum. The idea would be to assemble a set of prequalified DBEs that could create real value in that particular industry.[8] Then, buyers with explicit procurement opportunities would interview potential suppliers as the first step in the outsourcing process. This is a more focused approach than having hundreds (or thousands!) of diverse DBEs circulating around the convention center hoping for a lucky match, and supplier diversity professionals hanging around all day passing out trinkets and hoping there will be at least *one* potential match for the week.

Furthermore, traditional matchmaking has involved hosting a one-to-one conversation between buyers and sellers. But many DBEs are at an early stage of development and lack the scale to do major contract work alone. However, two DBEs working together—or a DBE working with an established majority corporate partner—might jointly have the capacity to do the contract work. But, due to historical exclusion, few DBEs have enough knowledge of the network to be able to identify potential strategic partners. This is an opportunity for visionary support organization to play a stronger role. Thus, *today, matchmaking is needed not only to bring buyers and sellers together but also to bring sellers and sellers together to create superior value for buyers.*

DECENTRALIZED OPERATIONS NEED UNIFORM QUALITY

In any nationwide organization, achieving uniform quality throughout the system is a challenge. The easy task is running headquarters-based activities, because there is high involvement and direct control. But elsewhere in the country, the organization is only as good as its local branch or affiliate.

The problem for nonprofits is that their work is labor-intensive but they have limited funding. Their effectiveness depends on their human capital, and it is hard to get top-rate staff at bottom-rate salaries. A basic thesis of labor economics is that you either pay more to hire people who are already trained and experienced, or you hire untrained, inexperienced people for less money and invest in their training and support. If you neither hire already-qualified staff nor train them, then your approach amounts to hoping for the best—and, usually, settling for widespread mediocrity.

Most support organizations that have satellite operations have uneven quality: there are some good field operations, and others that are not so good. As a result, some constituents receive good service, while others receive mediocre service.

What makes the biggest difference is the quality of leadership in the decentralized units. A good leader can do a lot with a limited payroll budget; a poor leader cannot do much with a generous budget.

Staff training is also a major determinant of success. A large percentage of the people who work in nonprofits are highly motivated to create a better world. But they need to know how to apply standardized instruments when diagnosing DBE needs, and they need to be able to draw on a broad network of support services. They are not expected to be all things to all people; they need to be able to identify the strengths and weaknesses of the diverse business and connect the owner with opportunities and with sources of help.

A good example of creating uniform competencies is the capacity building that was done by the MBDA, under its National Director, Ronald Langston. The MBDA had a budget that had shrunk under the Clinton and Bush administrations, while the population of MBEs to serve had been steadily growing. Staff members in the field organizations could not be paid much: the budget simply would not allow it. So Mr. Langston accepted the offer to partner with the Tuck School of Business at Dartmouth and arranged for everyone who directly or indirectly helped clients to participate in a week-long training program, and then to pass a competency test to ascertain their consulting skills. This initiative increased human capital by equipping staff members to tackle everyday client problems.

THE IDEAL SUPPORT ORGANIZATION

It is easy for organizations to lose focus on their core mission. They have to address the demands of various stakeholders, including those being served, those who provide funding, those who regulate the domain, and those who shape public opinion—as well as others. The influence attempts pull the organization in different directions.

Conflicting demands are dealt with not by a resolute leader but, rather, by a clear strategy. The core mission is usually embodied in the organization's name and echoed in its formal mission statement. The mission statement should proclaim a vision of what is possible if the organization succeeds. It is the guiding light that informs decision makers within the organization how they should choose among competing priorities.

The core strategy of a support organization should be to support diverse businesses. Everything else is secondary, including bending to the will of corporations or other entities that provide their funding. We would not, for example, call a support organization the "National Council to Showcase Minority Outsourcing." There is nothing wrong with showcasing DBE success stories, or highlighting a corporation's role in achieving those successes, but public relations is not the core mission of the support organization.

A true leader is the champion of the mission, showing how the mission can be implemented and inspiring efforts within the organization. But the leader's job is not done when all of the employees are pulling in the same direction. No support organization can have broad enough scope to tackle a system-level problem. A collaborative network needs to be mobilized if the mission is to succeed, which requires the leader to curtail interorganizational competition that has been sapping energy and blocking progress.

ADVOCACY SHOULD CREATE A FAVORABLE ENVIRONMENT FOR DBES

It is not enough to persuade public- or private-sector buyers to do business with diverse suppliers or go-to-market partners: the ideal support organization would insist that *the system* in which DBEs operate be adjusted to enable them to succeed.

So, in addition to advocating diverse participation goals—such as outsourcing to DBEs reflecting demographic proportions in the population—the ideal support organization would:

- push for changes in public policy that would require compliance with diverse outsourcing mandates;

- promote improvement of school systems to ensure the quality of the future minority workforce;

- lobby to preserve programs like 8(a), HUB Zone, and set-asides for historically disadvantaged groups;

- budget funds for business education, special training, and management and technical assistance; and

- persuade recalcitrant corporations to implement supplier diversity programs.

CERTIFICATION SHOULD BE UNIVERSAL AND USER-FRIENDLY

It is important that DBEs be certified. Once. The ideal support organization would ensure that certification be of high quality and universally accepted.

There is no added value to corporations, public-sector entities, or DBEs to be certified more than once—if it is done well the first time. So, in practice, the ideal support organization would work collaboratively with all other organizations to establish a national standard and pursue the efficiencies of centralized paperwork processing.

The ideal support organization would never depend on certification as a revenue stream. A "profit motive" would create the temptation to ensure that DBEs had to go to the time and trouble of getting certified by that particular organization, even if the DBE had been adequately certified by another organization.

At the same time, the ideal support organization would advocate the banning of self-certification and lobby for legislation that would make certification-related fraud a crime. It would advocate that all buyers accept reciprocal certification to the national high standard, irrespective of whether the certification came from its own certifying units or someone else's.

DBE BUSINESS PORTFOLIOS NEED TO BE BROAD

Some support organizations focus only on the corporate sector; others focus only on the public sector. While specialization has its advantages, the ideal support organization should be encouraging DBEs not to put all of their eggs in one basket. All sectors of the economy have their ups and downs, and DBEs' overreliance on a particular sector can spell ruin during a down cycle.

MATCHMAKING IS A PERPETUAL PROCESS, NOT AN EVENT

The ideal support organization would view matchmaking as an everyday process, not something that primarily happens once a year at an "opportunity exchange."

Done well, DBE matchmaking is more like facilitating dating than, say, hosting a craft fair. Fixing up friends involves assessing the basic compatibility between people who are available for dating, then connecting them with each other. Hosting a craft fair before Christmas involves providing tables and publicizing the event. In dating, the matchmaker's objective is the formation of a successful, ongoing relationship. The craft fair organizer's objective is to collect fees from the artisans, and she or he does not care whether the sellers make sales or the shoppers make purchases. The ideal support organization would do more than persuade corporations to buy booth space at its annual conventions and convince DBEs to pay the entry fees. It would foster the development of high-potential DBEs and promote these DBEs to buyers who needed the value they could add.

ACCESS TO CAPITAL NEEDS TO BE EASIER

Capital is often a constraining factor in DBE success. The ideal support organization would be advocating for government support of direct access to low-interest, government-backed loans, as well as performance bonds for DBEs in the construction industry. It would also be championing the formation and development of minority- and women-owned lending and private-equity institutions. It might even participate in the creation of capital cooperatives—entities that pool capital and risk for the benefit of businessmen and businesswomen whose access to capital is more difficult than for majority men.

DBE DEVELOPMENT NEEDS TO BE A TOP PRIORITY

In addition to helping DBEs with access to contracts and access to capital, the ideal support organization would help DBEs acquire the knowledge they need to achieve their full potential. Few support organizations provide learning experiences, and most that do cater to only a select few. Some support organizations actually have the word "development" in their names, yet they have done very little to develop their constituents. This is unfortunate, because *the right learning experiences can be transformational: they can put the high-potential DBE on the pathway to becoming a high-performing DBE.*

The ideal support organization would offer a high-quality learning experience as a basic benefit of membership. Then it would create, arrange, and monitor mentoring opportunities, realizing that the best mentoring may be done by other DBEs who are farther up the learning curve. It would also arrange for consulting, drawing on the resources of major corporations and sometimes taking advantage of the pro bono activities of major consulting firms, MBA programs, and civic organizations.

DEVELOPMENT OF SUPPORT ORGANIZATION CAPACITY IS IMPORTANT TOO

Support organization staff must be able to address the common challenges faced by the entrepreneurs they serve—such as having a clear strategy, maintaining viable cash flows, creating real customer value, and having an operations strategy that is aligned with customer requirements. Staff members throughout the support organization's decentralized system must be able to quickly diagnose these common shortcomings and point the DBE toward remedial action. That diagnostic capability can be acquired through training in basic consulting skills: providing that training would be a high priority in the ideal support organization.

SUPPORT ORGANIZATION ACTIVITIES NEED TO BE PRIORITIZED

Because the ideal support organization would not have an unlimited budget, each activity and expenditure would be scrutinized to assess alignment with the core mission, the likely impact, and the alternative uses of the same resources.

Key decision makers would have to justify allocations to a very demanding board, which would ask the following questions:

- Is there a better use for this allocation?
- Is this allocation consistent with our strategic priorities?
- What will the net impact be, and how will we measure it?
- Are we addressing our problem situation, or someone else's?
- Who else needs to be allied with us to help ensure that our efforts meet with success?

COLLABORATION IS ESSENTIAL TO CREATING REAL IMPACT

No single support organization is likely to have the influence, scope, or resources to create the system-wide changes that are needed to achieve economic parity. So support organizations need to work collaboratively with their natural allies. Many support organizations are working in isolation, jealously guarding their turf, and not making much of a difference. They would do well to learn from their counterparts in the environmental movement who work closely to achieve the common objectives of a healthy environment, retarding the pace of global warming, preventing species extinction, and fostering sustainability.

Natural allies ought to be working as allies; if they are not, then there is a failure of leadership.

LEADERSHIP IS A PIPELINE, NOT A PERSON

There is a big difference between a real leader and a cheerleader.

A real leader builds commitment and consensus among those who need to implement the strategy and make the vision a reality. In the realm of supplier diversity, cooperation is needed not just within the support organization but also within the broader support *system*, for the reasons explained earlier. A cheerleader, in contrast, urges people to compete hard. The cheerleader's own group is united by the presence of rivals, and the leader's contribution is to develop a strong sense of "us versus them." That is useful in some circumstances, but it is out of place in the supplier diversity movement. The challenge is so enormous that we cannot afford to divert energy from the core mission.

The most important responsibility of the board of a support organization is to appoint a good leader. But leadership succession is also important. Everyone knows that after a while, leaders and staff members fall into a routine, which leads to the phenomenon of doing the same things and hoping for different results. That is why so many appointments have term limits. The new leader comes in with fresh energy and fresh ideas and vigorously pursues the organization's mission. After a few years, all of those ideas have been implemented—or abandoned because they were infeasible—or the leader has become complacent, frustrated, or burned out. In any one of these scenarios, that is the point at which the leader ought to be grooming a successor to take over.

Here is the time line most people agree on. It takes a year to eighteen months to "get up to speed" in a leadership role. Within two years, it will be obvious whether the person who has taken on the leadership role is capable of doing the job. At that point, the board is responsible for either replacing the underperforming leader, or retaining and supporting the high-potential, high-achieving leader. In the latter case, by year five, the organization needs to be planning leadership succession.

Ideally, the next leader needs to be brought on board early enough so that he or she is ready to take over the reins by the time the organization is better off with new leadership. After eight years, a responsible board should be asking, why have we not replaced this leader? After ten years, it would be fair to raise the question of whether the board is carrying out its responsibility to the constituency.

CONCLUDING THOUGHTS

Historically, nonprofits and elected officials have led the fight for economic and social justice. Their courageous and valiant efforts paved the way for many minority entrepreneurs to take their place in the economic system, creating jobs and careers for millions of minorities and women. Support organizations should be praised for the positive changes that have occurred in our society due to their efforts, especially when one considers their limited resources and small budgets.

Today, support organizations are not doing enough. Minority population growth is outpacing the nation's success in including them in the economic mainstream. Unemployment, poverty, and social malaise are disproportionately high among minorities. Inner cities and poor rural areas are locked in cycles of hopelessness and despair. And the plight of one generation predisposes the next generation to share the same fate.

Fostering economic self-sufficiency is a proven antidote to these socioeconomic ills. Many minorities want to become entrepreneurs. It is in everyone's interest to foster their success, which is why support organizations play such a crucial role.

Support organizations must be keenly focused on their core mission. They must be effective and efficient. They must be collaborative. They must be well staffed and engaged in continuous improvement. And they must be strongly led, now and in the future.

The ideal organization we portrayed provides a template against which current support organizations can be assessed, and by which future support organizations can be designed. If the template does nothing more than stir up a debate over what the nation ideally needs, then it has served its purpose of focusing attention on what could be done to tackle the increasingly important problem of minority inclusion in the U.S. economy.

6   MINORITY BUSINESS SUCCESS REQUIRES LEADERSHIP AND DIRECTION

EXECUTIVE SUMMARY

Fostering the success of MBEs is a national priority, as this book has discussed in depth. The three major reasons can be summarized as follows:

1. We need to create jobs in order to ensure a vibrant economy and a substantial tax base. Broad economic participation is needed to support the swollen ranks of the retiring baby boom generation; to restore economic health to an economy crippled by the deepest recession since the Great Depression; to repay the debt incurred as a result of the economic stimulus outlays; and to provide goods and services domestically that would otherwise be purchased overseas, worsening the balance of payments.

2. Minorities are the fastest-growing sector of the population and are destined to become the future majority. But they have experienced a higher unemployment rate, accumulated less wealth, and made a smaller contribution to the entrepreneurial economy. As the U.S. position in the global economy continues to erode, this situation needs to change, for all of our sakes. Minorities will have to become the backbone of major supply chains as well as the core of

the entrepreneurial growth engine. The nation needs to foster their survival, prosperity, and growth to scale.

3. In our major cities and poor rural areas, minority-owned firms hire a higher proportion of minorities than do majority-owned firms. They create jobs and generate positive role models, career paths, and local wealth. They are the source of hope in many communities in which there has been little hope.

Thus we cannot continue to leave minorities on the sidelines of the economic mainstream. But a coordinated effort is required of the many parties that need to be fostering inclusion. The parties include legislators, supply chain managers in the public and private sectors, community leaders, support organizations, business schools, and public advocates across the political spectrum. They need to work together to create a different future, not as a liberal cause but, rather, as a national imperative. Everyone is worse off if minorities who could be contributing to economic progress are underperforming.

Dedicated people are making efforts, but not making much progress. The following are the ten most important things we can do to refocus our efforts to enhance minority economic participation.

1. Focus on economic prosperity and national competitive advantage.
2. Focus on MBE value creation in growth industries.
3. Focus MBEs on the lucrative sectors of value chains.
4. Focus attention on MBEs that are capable of becoming large employers.
5. Focus on development of MBEs rather than on procurement from MBEs.
6. Ensure adequate capitalization of high-potential MBEs.
7. Bolster public programs that foster minority business success.
8. Insist on uniform, multicategory certification that does not burden diverse businesses.
9. Measure what we need to achieve from supplier diversity programs.
10. Promote unity, leadership, and collaboration in the supplier diversity system.

These ten recommendations form the foundation for a new paradigm for fostering the success of minorities in the U.S. economy. The nation needs a different approach with stronger results—our children's and grandchildren's standard of living depends on our success in this endeavor, and MBEs are desperate for a system that works for them.

Public policy is in disarray. The various programs and laws that purport to advance the interests of MBEs do not complement each other and are not consistently enforced. Some even seem to have the perverse effect of penalizing minority success. Minorities lack the political cohesion needed to create the comprehensive public policy they need. But they are the fastest-growing sector of the voting public, and their interests are closely aligned with those of women, who are already the majority. Working together, minorities and women have the power; all that they need to advance their joint interests is leadership.

Supplier diversity initiatives also need to evolve. The supplier diversity movement has become viewed by critics as more "the establishment" than an agent of change, and fragmented and rigid at the moment in history when it needs to be collaborative and adaptive. Whether or not the frustration with the rate progress is justified, strong leadership is certainly needed to galvanize the various sources of support into a powerful force that will not settle for token accommodation but take us in a new direction and achieve real results.

To lead is to inspire zeal, focus, and commitment. The window of opportunity is open; we must seize the moment and create a different future for minorities in the U.S. economy.

MINORITY BUSINESS SUCCESS REQUIRES LEADERSHIP AND DIRECTION

The problem of minority economic underparticipation is at the system level, and it calls for a system-level solution. No organization or group, working alone, can bring about the changes that are necessary.

Coordinated responses, by definition, require coordination. Leadership is needed to align the various contributions that different entities can make. In the 1960s, the Reverend Martin Luther King Jr. gave focus, voice, and direction to the civil rights movement that achieved so much. Racism had been so deeply embedded in our national culture that it had persisted despite violating the principles set forth in the U.S. Constitution and the decisive outcome of the Civil War. Discrimination was institutionalized in our customs, laws, educational system, voting rights, and even our socially acceptable vocabulary: it was a violation of our national values and a disgrace to our founding principles. Inspired and guided by the leadership of Dr. King, people with a conscience stepped up to tear down barriers that were denying minorities access to the American Dream.

The same caliber of leadership is needed today to curtail *economic discrimination*. We need to address a deeply rooted, multifaceted set of constraints that are confining minorities and women to an economic role that is inconsistent with our national interest, thereby making the American Dream more elusive for all of us.

An effective leader will need to recognize the dynamics of the system, point the country in the right direction, persuade the establishment that it is in its self-interest to embrace change and become its champion, and insist that the various parties collaborate in achieving a multifaceted solution.

The leadership challenge is large. Dr. King had to confront a national culture that accepted social discrimination as "the way it is." Today's leaders have to confront a supplier diversity culture that has largely accepted the low priority most corporations and public entities give to supplier diversity as "the way it is."

Those most frustrated with the rate of progress would charge that many people in supplier diversity are making a comfortable living promoting the status quo. They are following the prescribed standard operating procedures, attending the circuit's events, celebrating each other's limited accomplishments, and enjoying the prestige of serving a noble cause while achieving little long-term impact. As a result, critics say, *the supplier diversity establishment has become as much a part of the problem as a part of the solution*. Their activity, although largely ineffectual, actually reduces the impetus to develop an innovative, comprehensive solution that creates real inclusion.

If the critique is mistaken, then critics owe the supplier diversity movement an apology. If the critique is valid, then the supplier diversity movement owes the country a better effort, because the problem is certainly growing faster than the solutions we have been applying. The proportion of minorities in the population is increasing at an increasing rate. But minorities still have less lifetime earning potential, higher unemployment, and lower family wealth than their majority counterparts. As a result of the continuing disparity in economic inclusion, we lose national competitive advantage against rival economies; recovery from recession is impaired; already-daunting urban problems are exacerbated; and precious public funds get diverted from investment in infrastructure, research and development, and fostering the development of important industry clusters.

This is not someone else's problem: it is ours. And it is not about assigning blame: it is about creating a different future.

Simply put, the nation is not doing enough to address the issues that are darkening our horizon. There are over 4 *million* minority businesses in the United States. Only a fraction receives any help at all. The SBA has been decimated by budget cuts. The MBDA is a skeleton of what it was during the Nixon administration. Very few corporations have significant supplier diversity programs, and few of those that do give MBEs important value-chain roles. Meanwhile, business schools that purport to be at the cutting edge are overlooking the fastest-growing sector of the entrepreneurial economy. None of the support organizations provides the certification and development services that its constituency needs. And the tendency to focus on spending level rather than impact dooms most diverse inclusion efforts to be more of a philanthropic donation than an investment in long-term competitive advantage at the value-chain level.

If we do nothing different, the supplier diversity movement risks falling into obscurity. Already we are losing momentum, for two reasons.

First, many people misinterpret the visible progress that minorities have made in high-profile areas as evidence that there is no longer much of a diversity problem. We elected an African American president, minorities permeate entertainment and professional sports, and minorities and women are in a few high-visibility executive and board positions. The majority of the general public does not read economic statistics or spend time in inner cities: they watch television and read about celebrities in *People* magazine, and they erroneously conclude that discrimination and economic disparities are things of the past.

Second, the relentless attacks on programs designed to foster economic inclusion have reversed some of the progress we have made since the Civil Rights Act. The ultraconservative message is phrased as an appeal for "fair treatment," portraying affirmative action, 8(a), and other ameliorative programs as an infringement on others' rights. This is where strong leadership could make a big difference in shaping both public opinion and the actions of policy makers. The public is exposed to a barrage of anti-minority and anti-feminist messages on hate radio and right-wing, extremist-owned television: a respected leader's voice is needed to put those views into a perspective that has greater accuracy and more balance.

WE HAVE A HISTORIC OPPORTUNITY
We are in an era of change. Historians will look back on the present years and compare them to the 1960s. Both will be seen as eras of discontent—times in which a critical mass longed for a different approach and was willing to step up and do something about it.

Today, the restlessness and openness to new directions are evident across age and gender, with educated professionals particularly likely to take action to advance progressive causes. The Internet facilitates concerted action among widely distributed grassroots activists, who can mobilize other sympathizers with the stroke of a key. These are people who have connections to spheres of influence, knowledge of how institutions operate, and networks of potential allies in their causes. They need leadership to focus their efforts on achieving specific, meaningful, and impactful changes. They are an army waiting to be mobilized.

We need to lead supplier diversity in a new direction. The following ten steps will greatly accelerate our progress.

Recommendation I: Focus On Economic Prosperity and National Competitive Advantage
The United States lacks a National Industrial Strategy. Rival nations display a stronger sense of direction. They know what industries they

want to dominate, retain, or abandon; what industry clusters must remain intact to ensure value-chain integrity; what workforces are needed to staff those industry clusters; and how revenue streams will be generated and recirculated to create vibrant local, regional, and sectoral[1] economies.

While rival nations have been systematically targeting, infiltrating, and then picking off our industries, ideologues—backed by lobbyists whose clients stand to gain at the country's expense—have been urging the country to ignore the exodus of revenues, jobs, and whole industries. Their loud voices have drowned out thoughtful debate about what is in the national interest by invoking various "isms"—protectionism, socialism, even communism—all to their country's detriment. The glib negativity succeeds in driving a wedge into American public opinion, but it fails to address the problem of economic erosion that is looming larger and larger.

The economy is staggering from a body blow that resulted from the underregulation that had been advocated by these same strident ideologues. Millions of jobs have moved overseas. Unemployment has hit a record high. We have been mired in the worst recession since the Great Depression. We have lost much of our preeminence in education, innovation, finance, and technology. And, as a result, the national standard of living had dropped precipitously even before the meltdown of our financial system.

Meanwhile, the sector of the population that has been saddled with the highest rates of educational deficiency and unemployment, and the lowest rates of wealth accumulation, is growing at a rate that will make it the majority within a few decades.

The trajectory makes our standard of living unsustainable. We need the full economic contribution of all of the working population and all of the entrepreneurial community. It is a national imperative, yet the issue gets misconceived as a social program. If the country had been invaded by a military force, and we were gradually ceding territory—first California, then Oregon, then Washington, and so on—then we would pay attention to the big picture, stop squabbling over ideological distractions, enlist whoever can contribute to the war effort, and mobilize our resources to preserve the country. If, instead, the country has been invaded economically, and we are gradually ceding markets—first textiles, then consumer electronics, then automobiles, and so on—then we should pay attention to the big picture, stop squabbling over ideological distractions, ensure the contributions of those who have been underparticipating in the economy, and mobilize our resources to foster their inclusion and success.

The time is ripe for strong leadership to frame the problem of minority exclusion as an economic issue with national competitive advantage at stake.

Many people were disappointed that minority inclusion did not become a front-burner issue when the country inaugurated its first black president. But we have to be realistic: the new administration inherited two wars, the deepest recession since the Great Depression, nuclear proliferation, a broken national health care system, rogue nations, and myriad other pressing problems. In that context, perhaps the administration should have been forgiven for not giving minority inclusion top priority. But it needs to get *some* priority, which is unlikely to happen if we remain starved of the leadership and voice that the supplier diversity movement needs.

The leadership role includes:

- being the respected public voice of the movement;
- couching the minority economic inclusion challenge in terms of national prosperity and national competitive advantage;
- shaping public policy decisions to promote full economic participation;
- articulating the business case for corporate supplier diversity;
- persuading the minority- and women-serving institutions that have become complacent or self-serving to refocus on their core mission;
- integrating the efforts of the various contributors to progress; and
- arbitrating the petty turf battles that sap energy from the cause.

The movement will never achieve real impact unless we can speak with a strong, unified voice about the magnitude of the problem; the feasibility, costs, and benefits of the alternative solutions; and the steps that need to be taken.

Recommendation 2: Focus on MBE Value Creation in Growth Industries

Strategic choice begins with minority business owners assessing their core competency and resources and then identifying the opportunities to create value in different industries. Their choices are growing industries, mature industries, and dying industries. And, over time, all growing industries mature and then decline.

If minority business owners find themselves in a low-revenue industry, then they might be able to adjust their offerings to create value in a high-revenue industry. For example, can an MBE that has been designing print advertising design Web pages instead? Can an MBE that rebuilds generators and electric motors for the automotive industry service wind farms? Can a translation company that specializes in Spanish become a Hispanic marketing company? Can an MBE that services mechanized farming equipment perform maintenance, repair, and overhaul on a military base?

While growth industries are ideal for minority involvement because of their longer-term potential, particular mature industries may be almost as good if they are stable during economic downturns. Much government work is stable across economic conditions compared to, say, luxury goods. Larger-scale construction and other infrastructure maintenance and improvement projects often have long cycles that span recessions, and these ought to be opportunities for MBEs. Military bases tend to have needs that are stable over long periods, in contrast to cutting-edge weapons programs, which can end as suddenly as they are begun. And utilities and health care involve steady demand, although the prudent minority business owner will pay close attention to developments in the regulatory environment.

While the basic responsibility for choosing a promising industry rests with MBEs, institutions that support them can help guide their transition. Many business owners left their previous employer because they saw an entrepreneurial opportunity in that particular industry and simply do not know that their core competencies are applicable in other industries that offer more promise. They need help in seeing what is possible—and where the high-revenue, high-growth opportunities lie.

Recommendation 3: Focus MBEs on the Lucrative Sectors of Value Chains

Even if MBEs do not get stuck in a low-potential industry, they often get stuck in a low-potential link of the value chain. More often still, they are relegated to an unimportant support role on the periphery.

This happens because purchasing agents perceive a lot of risk and little reward in transferring business from an existing majority supplier to an unknown new supplier.[2] The notoriety of a bad outsourcing decision is highest in the case of strategic suppliers—those that are involved in the central value chain who can contribute to the corporation's competitive advantage if they perform well and create competitive disadvantage if they perform poorly. The understandable response is to allocate inconsequential business to MBEs.

A better approach is to give the highest-potential MBEs an important role in the value chain and then do everything possible to ensure their success. But thoughtless incentive structures in old-school organizations discourage strategic judgment. If the outsourcing manager is held accountable for simply achieving diversity-spend targets, then the expeditious way to achieve them is to offer contracts that are unimportant to the functioning of the organization. Such contract offerings might include janitorial services, low-level IT, staffing, printing, industrial supplies, giveaways, and the like. Minorities can easily enter these supply domains because there are low barriers to entry. But what makes it easy for one minority business to enter these domains makes it easy for hundreds, or even thousands, of diverse businesses, which bid down the price and drive out the profit potential. This approach does not create inclusion; rather, it perpetuates *exclusion* from major value chains.

It does not take much imagination to visualize what happens when the supplier diversity establishment endorses this approach by giving the strongest accolades to the organizations doing the most such outsourcing. The impact on wealth creation and accumulation in minority communities is low: revenue streams are unstable and profit margins are low as a result of many minority suppliers jostling for short-term contracts—and short-term survival. And *we end up with a ghettoized diverse supplier base and supplier diversity professionals viewed as strategically irrelevant.*

We need a paradigm shift, because the supplier diversity establishment has institutionalized this approach, trapping minorities and women in an arrangement that appears to be for their benefit but in practice legitimizes their economic marginalization.

Recommendation 4: Focus Attention on MBEs That Are Capable of Becoming Large Employers

Most MBEs are very small: only about 5 percent have annual revenues over $100,000, plus one or more employees on the payroll. Some of them are "lifestyle businesses'—entrepreneurial ventures that will allow the owner the freedom to be self-employed. But these will not create a lot of jobs, accumulate wealth that can be reinvested to create business growth, or attract supplier firms to locate nearby and form a local industry cluster. And they will not be of sufficient scale to participate in the global economy.

The economy needs MBEs to be involved in medium- and large-scale enterprises; MBEs need help growing to scale.

There are three options to achieve the scale necessary for inclusion in major value chains: organic growth, mergers and acquisitions, and strategic alliances. Organic growth is the lowest-risk approach, but it is slow and requires a series of transformations that the minority business owner may not be capable of implementing. Acquisition is a viable strategy if the financial resources are available, and if the owner has the spare time and management talent available to run a second enterprise—and, to manage the integration process. Strategic alliance is the most promising growth strategy because it does not incur the same financial burden or size penalties. But entrepreneurial personalities tend to be reluctant to give up the control necessary to operate under a collaborative, negotiated arrangement.

Leaders must have a vision of minority executives running larger-scale enterprises, and they must be resourceful in making their vision a reality.

We usually think about matchmaking between buyers and sellers; we also need to think about matchmaking between minority businesses that ought to be working together to create scale and scope. We probably will need to place some thoughtful bets on minorities that can handle a strategic acquisition and help them ante up the capital needed to close the deal.

Before we move on, we should note the paradox that although the economy needs minorities to prosper and grow their businesses, we sometimes create disincentives. In the defense sector, for example, public policy places an emphasis on small rather than diverse businesses, and economically deprived rather than affluent business owners. The arguments in favor of that policy are that small business is the backbone of the U.S. economy and that the economy as a whole benefits from channeling dollars into that sector; and, it is more equitable to help out poorer people rather than to give more to people who are already wealthy.

But there is an unintended downside. The policy has the effect of penalizing success. Take the case of a very promising entrepreneur who has the potential to succeed in providing value to customers, growing the business, and creating wealth and jobs in the local community. This particular entrepreneur is a Hispanic or an African American woman who, compared to a white male presenting the same business case, has a lower probability of being approved for a loan and would pay higher interest rates if the loan were granted. If she is successful financially despite the bias, and her net worth rises above lower-middle-class standards, then business is taken away from her because she no longer qualifies as poor. If she is successful in terms of growth, creating jobs and wealth in the inner city, then business is taken away from her because she is no longer small. Neither the public interest nor corporate self-interest is served by using these simple measures of eligibility for support.

Recommendation 5: Focus on Development of MBEs Rather Than on Procurement from MBEs

If we approach supplier diversity efforts from a traditional procurement perspective, then the focus is on diverting some contracts to diverse suppliers while getting at least the same value that would be obtained from majority suppliers. This approach is wrongheaded.

A more enlightened twenty-first-century perspective is to view out-sourcing as a substitute for insourcing—being supplied by one of the or-ganization's own internal divisions. In the relentless quest for competitive advantage, executives would want their own divisions to deliver maxi-mum value. To achieve this, they would audit the division's effectiveness and invest in its success by providing resources, consulting help, training, and oversight. Because the consequences for organizational effectiveness are the same, it is logical to make similar investments in development whether outsourcing or insourcing.

Supplier diversity needs to be seen as having a strategic role in corpo-rations and public-sector agencies. To gain that status, the "Holy Grail" of supplier diversity—the business case—must be made in terms of enhanc-ing competitive advantage at the value-chain level. In an era of outsourc-ing, companies no longer compete with other companies; rather, inte-grated value chains compete with rival value chains, often in the global marketplace. *Investing in the development of suppliers strengthens the or-ganization's ability to deliver value and defeat competitors.* That is the business case.

Success in developing MBEs requires a coordinated, multifaceted effort tailored to the different needs of different-size MBEs operating in particu-lar industries. Some various facets of a comprehensive program of MBE development follow.

- Adequate educational support should be made available to minority entrepreneurs, owners of minority businesses that have growth potential, and executives of larger minority-owned enterprises. Currently, the major business schools are doing virtually nothing to help MBEs; support organizations are not providing the level of educational support that their constituency needs; corporations and public-sector agencies are defining MBE development as beyond their mission[3]; and governments are not providing adequate learning experiences, in some cases hoping that low-cost distance learning will accomplish something it was never designed to do.

- Organizations that have a problem with insourcing bring in consul-tants to remedy the performance deficit. When the same functions are outsourced, many act as though the problem does not affect them. High-quality consulting help can be provided by firms such as Accenture; but help does not only come from firms of that caliber. The Kauffman Foundation provides highly competent coaches to minority businesses that need help. The SBA arranges consultations with retired executives through its SCORE program. A handful of business schools arranges for teams of MBA students to assist fledgling businesses. These examples reflect a growing public-service ethic: many people are willing to make a societal contribution and only need to be steered toward an opportunity to make a difference. We need to be resourceful in bringing MBEs and experts together.

- Mentoring is a way of moving minority business owners quickly up the learning curve: basically, the more experienced business owner shares insights with the less experienced. Mentoring can be extremely helpful, but it does not happen as often as it should. Few formal mentoring programs are effective when the organizations have no motive other than contract compliance; programs that are most effective arise from a commitment to MBE success and are supplemented with an educational component. But we should note that entrepreneurs tend to be self-reliant and therefore hesitant to reach out for help. Ironically, many potential mentors are usually quite willing to give back, especially to members of their own minority community, but they need to be matched with MBEs who can benefit from their help.

- An advisory board can accelerate the development of minority suppliers. Outsiders bring a different perspective and have experience and connections that can benefit the MBE. If all they do is ask intelligent questions, then the minority business owner will be better off. There are myriad talented people looking for opportunities to make a difference; some entity needs to connect those willing to help with those who would benefit from it.

In sum, if we emphasize development, then a broad range of possibilities can emerge. Some of the options cost nothing; others will yield benefits that far exceed costs. But the sophisticated outsourcing manager ought to look beyond cost/benefit and consider strategic advantage. Old-school procurement is based on the assumption that the department issuing the specifications knows best. Leading-edge outsourcing managers assume that the supplier knows best. That is why they outsource work that a supplier can do better than they can accomplish in-house. Suppliers know their industry. And they know what is possible, which may be better than what the purchasing agent is asking for.

In sum, if they are developed, minority suppliers can have a positive impact on competitive advantage, not just on the cost of goods sold.

Recommendation 6: Ensure Adequate Capitalization of High-Potential MBEs

As we have noted and documented, minorities, like women, have a lower probability of securing funding for their businesses, and they pay higher interest rates if they do receive the funding. This is an unacceptable situation, because it is in the national interest for them to survive, prosper, and grow to scale. So we need to think creatively about the alternative sources of capital.

The easiest and most obvious way to help MBEs with their capital needs is to make sure they get paid on time. Cash flow is often a major problem. Minorities tend to have less to pledge as collateral, so they often have to resort to high-cost borrowing—for example, using their credit cards—to finance the shortfall between cash outlays and cash receipts.

Many corporations and public-sector purchasers are unaware of what really goes on when they impose payment terms that favor their own organizations. In effect, the big organizations are using their purchasing clout to force struggling businesses to be unwilling lenders. This bullying is not fair; but worse, it is ultimately self-defeating. Major organizations need strong supply chains. If they weaken suppliers by forcing them to accept payment terms that sap the suppliers' vitality, then they are hurting themselves in the long run. The major organizations almost always have a lower cost of capital than their MBE suppliers: therefore, *it makes economic sense to pay invoices when the supplier needs the money.*

Even if the MBE is being paid on time, capital infusions may be needed. Accordingly, a mechanism that has been used to sustain smaller businesses is to have governmental agencies guarantee loans. But this approach has had limited success: it still leaves the decision of whether to grant the loan to the loan officer of a private-sector lending institution, whose motives may not be aligned with public policy. This can lead to a situation where funds are available and the loan has been guaranteed, but the loan officer will not release the funds. As a result, the public interest is thwarted. *It is time to consider arrangements for making direct loans to diverse business owners whose success will benefit the economy and the country.*

Providing equity investment is an alternative way of helping MBEs develop in scale and scope. It is an attractive alternative to debt financing when assets are fully leveraged and further debt is going to adversely affect the MBE's capital structure. The downside is that the entrepreneur has to give up some control. Furthermore, when the minority business owner gives up more than 51 percent equity, he or she is likely to give up MBE status. Nevertheless, equity financing is an option worth considering by many MBEs and by the entities that support and do business with them.

The most urgent need for a different system is in the construction industry. We are reiterating this point because this is an industry in which minorities ought to be able to fully participate.

Minorities encounter two barriers in the construction industry. They need access to capital for growth and fund work in process, just like any other business. But they also need to post performance bonds—which amount to insurance coverage to compensate their customer if they underperform on their contract. In practice, the bonding requirement poses a barrier to entry. So if government agencies want to create jobs in communities with large concentrations of minorities, they can provide the bonding, create risk pools, or guarantee the bonds the same way they guarantee loans. Or they can change the law, or perhaps provide waivers.

Governments can also help ease the financial difficulties of minorities in the construction industry by helping to protect them from the predatory contractor practices. Large construction companies have the power to impose unfavorable contract terms as well as the legal acumen to get small subcontractors to agree to terms that they do not fully understand. The minority subcontractors may perform on the contract in good faith yet still encounter a refusal to pay. The MBEs are unlikely to have the resources to press their claims in court, or to cope with the payment delays that attend a dispute. *It would be in the public interest for governments to provide an ombudsperson to resolve disputes expeditiously and fairly.* Helping the minority firm avoid the cash flow deficit is at least as good as providing a loan to make up for it. And ensuring justice is always better than alleviating the impact of exploitative practices.

Recommendation 7: Bolster Public Programs that Foster Minority Business Success

Government plays an essential role in fostering the nation's commercial activities. Increasingly, this requires ensuring that diverse businesses survive, prosper, and grow to scale, because these enterprises are an increasingly important component of the economy.

We need to bolster public policy and the public agencies that implement it.

The public policy most in need of bolstering involves inclusion mandates. They continue to be under attack, despite their record of achievement. Everyone should realize by now that reserving a small portion of "set-aside" business for groups that have faced past discrimination—and who need to be contributing to gross domestic product rather than being a drag on the economy—is wise public policy. Set-aside programs give these groups a chance to establish a track record. If they perform well, then they will earn future contracts; if they perform poorly, then they will not. Set-asides give them "a chance at bat."

It is also in the national interest to use set-aside mechanisms to draw business into geographic areas that have a high poverty rate. If we want to create economic self-sufficiency in inner cities and poor rural communities, then it makes sense to provide these communities with business opportunities. The alternative is to pay for unemployment compensation and increased public services. It is better to foster minority businesses, thereby creating positive role models in distressed communities. Conservative pundits will always be able to point to examples where good public policy led to bad outcomes, but *the weight of evidence supports the wisdom of government continuing to use set-aside programs to shape local economies*, and to create opportunities for talented, industrious minorities to succeed.[4]

Unsuccessful in fully eliminating inclusion mandates, right-wing extremists have sought to cripple the government agencies that implemented them, and they have done serious damage during the past two decades. As a result, the government agencies we have in place to implement the programs are inadequate. They are underfunded, understaffed, and fragmented, and they lack the teeth to ensure compliance with policy directives. They need to be rebuilt with a stronger focus.

The U.S. Department of Commerce, which has a stewardship responsibility to maintain America's place in the global economy, needs to set the overall strategic direction. Its most important contribution will be to articulate a National Industrial Strategy that identifies nationally important industries and prescribes the industry clusters and infrastructure needed to make them successful. The full economic participation of minorities and women will be an essential component of that strategy.[5]

The capacity of the U.S. Small Business Administration needs to be restored so that it can implement its programs. The SBA should continue to focus on start-up and fledgling businesses and to administer targeted interventions such as the HUB Zone and 8(a) programs. But to accomplish its mission, the SBA needs to replace the workforce that was disbanded during the Bush administration. Furthermore, the SBA creates impact through a large decentralized system of client-facing service providers who must be trained to function effectively as consultants and financial advisors.

The MBDA's role should be refocused to supplement rather than replicate what the SBA does. It should serve *established* minority-owned businesses that can be grown to scale. The MBDA should be structured like a major consulting firm, and its processes need to be reengineered to reflect its sharper strategic focus.

Other agencies have important, complementary roles to play—for example, the U.S. Department of Labor is concerned with the national workforce; the U.S. Department of Agriculture is concerned with rural poor communities; the U.S. Department of Health and Human Services is concerned with the economic self-sufficiency of disadvantaged communities; and the U.S. Department of Interior is responsible for the well-being of Native American communities. These and other sister agencies need to be working in concert with each other. If we add in state and local governments, then we have a complex network of stakeholders and service providers whose efforts need to be coordinated to achieve maximum impact.

The need for integration of the various programs is so great that the White House would be remiss if it failed to appoint a *Special Assistant to the President for Diverse Business*. The assignment would be to provide horizontal coordination and to ensure that the special needs of population subgroups are met, as well as to ensure role alignment and collaboration. (This vital leadership role is discussed in more detail in Recommendation 10.)

Recommendation 8: Insist On Uniform, Multicategory Certification that Does not Burden Diverse Businesses

Certification has gone awry.

Certification is—or should be—a service to diverse businesses. It assures decision makers in public- and private-sector procurement that these are legitimate diverse businesses, not front companies. It is a defense against fraudulent representations. But certification has become a source of revenue for support organizations and a source of jobs for public-sector employees, sometimes at the expense of the struggling minority- or woman-owned business.

Here is the exemplar of the problem. A dark-skinned African American woman business owner was certified as a WBE but had to go through certification a second time as an MBE. Then she had to be certified a third time as a veteran, despite having received a Purple Heart for sustaining combat wounds. The city authorities would not accept any of those certifications to do city work, so she had to get certified a fourth time—and then a fifth time by the state so that she could do work outside of the city limits.

In this example, the public interest and corporate interests are not being served by multiple certifications: one high-quality certification would have prevented fraud and allowed this poor MWBE to spend her time and effort working on her business. The only people benefiting from this arrangement are the certifying authorities that collect the fees from paperwork that has already been done by someone else. *Collectively, they stood in the way of the MBE getting business that everyone wanted to give her.*

Everyone except the certifying authorities is calling for universal, multicategory certification to a high standard. Its time has come. But it bears repeating that the various differences *must not* be collapsed into a single category—a "diverse business enterprise." That would prevent targeting particular groups, such as women, minorities, veterans, Native Americans, businesses located in HUB Zones, and so on, for inclusion mandates. *We need one certification, not one category.*

Recommendation 9: Measure What We Need to Achieve from Supplier Diversity Programs

The goals of supplier diversity programs are

- to help minority businesses survive, prosper, and grow to scale;
- to create jobs;
- to provide role models in inner cities;
- to create career paths for people who would otherwise probably work in dead-end jobs; and
- to generate individual and community wealth.

The goal is not to divert accounts payable to certified diverse businesses. It is to have impact. Yet we only *measure* diversity-spend. So that is what we tend to get.

As we have noted, the easy way to achieve diversity-spend is to offer contracts that are unimportant to the functioning of the organization. That way, there is low risk arising from dealing with unfamiliar suppliers. The traditional approach is to issue an RFQ for a nonessential commodity item and then award the fixed-term contract to the lowest of the diverse bidders.

We need a paradigm shift, because the supplier diversity establishment has institutionalized this approach, in many cases trapping minorities and women in an arrangement that appears to be for their benefit but in practice legitimizes their exclusion.

A cynic's view of "how supplier diversity works" is harsh, and perhaps largely unfair, but it nevertheless gives us some insights about how inappropriate measurement can obscure the core mission:

The corporation yields to pressure to create a supplier diversity program. A manager is appointed, with a written mandate from the CEO to achieve a diversity-spend goal. Managers throughout the corporation are coerced into offering up some contract volume to diverse businesses, or else face performance-review penalties. The supplier diversity manager then works with the managers and purchasing agents to identify noncritical purchases that can be steered toward minorities. RFQs are issued and contracts awarded to MBEs until the diverse purchase volume equals the diversity-spend goal.

Meanwhile, the corporation has made appropriate donations to the support organizations and is eligible for awards that reflect both diversity-spend and the level of donation. The award recipients are chosen by a jury of their peers—supplier diversity professionals who are following the same standard operating procedures. The supplier diversity people even pay for the elaborate black-tie events that celebrate each other's achievements.

Nobody is asking whether these corporate programs are making a real difference or whether the money could have been better spent. And while all of the pageantry is going on, most diverse suppliers remain on the periphery of the major value chains.

This jarring, but often-repeated, critique brings two issues into sharp focus: What *impact* is a supplier diversity program supposed to achieve, and how do we know when it has been achieved? Remember that the business case for supplier diversity focuses on developing supply chain capacity and creating wealth within emerging domestic markets. The business case is not supported by counting up the dollar volume of business placed with MBEs.

If we were to measure impact rather than diversity-spend, we would gain by helping MBEs who need help and by creating a different future for a set of U.S. citizens who never had a fair chance to achieve the American Dream.

Helping disadvantaged MBEs in disadvantaged communities creates impact. But not every MBE is disadvantaged, or from a disadvantaged community. Consider the differences within the following set of minority business enterprises:

A. A business located in an inner city founded and run by an African American or a Hispanic entrepreneur with a workforce drawn from the inner city

B. A business owned by a minority that employs few minorities but places most of its outsourcing (second-tier spend) with minority businesses

C. An IT business set up in the United States by a highly educated immigrant from India who outsources all of the work to the successful, established family business back in Hyderabad

D. A company that had been a white male-owned business until an African American sports celebrity bought a 51 percent equity interest in it, resulting in no changes except for the equity structure

E. An established company that has been thriving for many years without customers being aware that it is owned and operated by a minority

The "diversity-spend" resulting from doing business with each of these MBEs has very different consequences in terms of the core mission, or the business case for supplier diversity.

A high-quality certification would ascertain that the company in Scenario A should be eligible for and deserving of set-aside contracts. The public and corporate interests are served when jobs are created in inner cities and the local economy is stimulated by the re-spending of income streams in the community. The experience the inner-city residents get by working in this business strengthens the labor pool.

In Scenario B, the economic impact is just as strong, but it would be important to measure "second-tier diversity-spend" to realize that doing business preferentially with this MBE achieves the underlying goal.

It is hard to make a case for preferential access to contracts in Scenario C. Even though this business is minority owned and operated, it does not seem to be a disadvantaged business, and it is impairing American prosperity rather than bolstering it. Corporate interests may be served by taking advantage of the lower labor rates in India, but the public interest is not served when jobs are exported overseas.

It is also hard to make a case for preferential access to contracts in Scenario D, but for different reasons. It is a good thing that the successful minority athlete has made an investment to sustain personal wealth, but the benefits are all accruing to the individual. There is no social or economic benefit to allocating business to this particular MBE, although corporations may gain a favorable image in the minority community by publicizing their association with this celebrity.

Scenario E shows a situation in which certification creates no benefits to the minority-owned business but benefits corporations that are striving to achieve diversity-spend targets. In that scenario, the supplier diversity function is not creating jobs, wealth, career paths, or role models in disadvantaged communities; nor is it strengthening the value chain. It is scrubbing the corporate data banks to uncover diverse spend within accounts payable records. It represents business that was placed with the MBE without any effort or influence from the supplier diversity professionals. There is nothing unethical about doing this to create a total picture of where corporate funds are being spent, but there is nothing laudable about it either.

These hypothetical scenarios show that if we want to create impact, then getting people certified as MBEs and then measuring spend level is an imperfect way to go about achieving our goals. It seems inevitable that sooner or later we will have to adopt a multifaceted scorecard for shaping policies and assessing the effectiveness of supplier diversity efforts.[6]

We need to point out that despite the possible shortcomings of the traditional accounts-payable-to-DBEs metric, *we applaud organizations that have achieved high levels of diversity-spend*. The Billion Dollar Roundtable honors the highest achievers on this dimension, and rightly so. These are the corporations that have been among the most committed to the success of diverse businesses.

But to emphasize how imperfect diversity-spend is as a measure, consider the following two cases and then decide which one is the more deserving of public accolades:

- A corporation with $100 billion in annual sales outsources $3 billion to minority businesses
- A corporation with $1 billion in annual sales outsources $300 million to minority businesses

The first corporation has the bigger impact on the minority business community, allocating 3 percent of its outsourcing volume; the second is trying harder, allocating 30 percent of its outsourcing—proportional to the percentage of minorities in the U.S. population. Both corporations deserve accolades, but for different reasons. The examples show the need for a more sophisticated approach to measurement.

Recommendation 10: Promote Unity, Leadership, and Collaboration in the Supplier Diversity System

Complex challenges require complex interventions. Think of building a school, recovering from a disaster, or fighting a war. Success in each of those situations requires not just good performance from each of the various contributors but coordination of their efforts into an integrated response.

The costs of inadequate *performance* by any of the contributors are high in each of these cases. Roofs collapse; the evacuation vehicles are not staged; and the enemy is allowed to take the strategic high ground. But the costs of inadequate *coordination* can nullify everyone's best efforts: the school does not get completed by the start of the school year; the evacuation routes are not cleared to let the rescue vehicles through; and the enemy air defenses are not suppressed in time, leaving our aircraft vulnerable and our ground troops unsupported.

In this book, we are not concerned with construction, disaster recovery, or modern warfare. We are concerned with economic inclusion and national competitive advantage. But the parallels are clear enough to highlight the importance of strong leadership in each of these complex situations. We are building an entrepreneurial economy; helping people whose lives have been devastated by discrimination, chronic poverty, and now recession; and fighting for our national standard of living against global competitors.

We have seen that *isolated efforts consume resources without making much of a difference.* Certainly there are some success stories. We celebrate the minority entrepreneur who was raised in the projects but who goes on to establish a business that provides jobs in the local community. And we celebrate the woman who was raised to believe she could only become a secretary, a nurse, or a teacher but who goes on to found a successful enterprise. But we need to recognize that these are the exceptions: most minorities and women are doomed to remain spectators rather than participants in the mainstream economy.

It is heartening to see the cornerstone being laid at a new charter school but disheartening to know that the school was founded to escape the numbing constraints of a dysfunctional school district. It is heartening to see a helicopter plucking a flood victim off of her roof but disheartening to know that others drowned or are left homeless because of administrative chaos. And it is heartening to learn that our soldiers fought their way out of an ambush but disheartening to learn that they were ambushed because the various intelligence services did not cooperate with each other.

Success requires coordination. And coordination requires leadership.

In the case of minority economic inclusion, there are at least a dozen different functions that need to be carried out. A sample listing is offered in the left column of Table 6.1. Here is the rationale for including this set of functions:

- Different size minority businesses need different kinds of help. A start-up is very different from an established business that is growing. And a big business is qualitatively different from a smaller, growing business.

- Entrepreneurs usually know how to deliver a service or manufacture a product much better than they know how to run a business. Providing entrepreneurial training dramatically increases their chance of success. But different skills are needed to run large businesses—and the entrepreneur who is good at founding new businesses may be hopeless at running large-scale enterprises. So we also need to train minorities to become the executives who run businesses of scale.

TABLE 6.1

Worksheet to Assess Adequacy of MBE Support

(Fill in your estimate of how well MBEs are being served by each potential source of help.)

Focus of Attention[a] \ Source of Help	SBA	MBDA	Support Organizations	Advocacy Organizations	Political Entities	Business Schools
Minority Start-ups						
High Growth Potential Minority Firms						
Large-Scale Minority Businesses						
Entrepreneurial Training						
Minority Executive Development						
Minority Workforce Development						
Development of a Local Economy						
Access to Capital						
Government Contracting						
Corporate Outsourcing						
Shaping Public Policy						
Matchmaking: Supplier Alliances						

[a]Certification is not included in the table because it is not a value-added activity, it is only an audit. MBEs do not become better suppliers as a result of certification; everyone is better off because high-quality certification discourages fraud attempts. Some support organizations and governmental units have made certification their primary focus when they could be devoting more effort to developing MBEs and otherwise improving minority inclusion and economically distressed communities. They argue that it is not their job to help create a brighter future for minorities. But cynics point out that the supplier diversity establishment that provides their funding has a stake in maintaining the status quo and wants them to be narrow service providers, not change agents.

- A major benefit of promoting minority business ownership is the tendency of MBEs to hire minorities in greater proportion than is typical of white-owned businesses. But the minority workforce needs to be trained too, otherwise the MBE will not be able to compete, retain customers, or get positive referrals.

- A local economy depends on one or more core businesses, plus an industry cluster that allows the core business to function—as well as various entrepreneurial businesses that provide a support network and the necessary infrastructure. Without all of these elements, the core business is not viable and will move or close. And all of these elements are necessary for revenues to recirculate in the local economy, creating wealth and jobs by a multiplier effect.

- Minority businesses need capital, just like any other business. But minorities have a harder time acquiring it. If we need MBEs to succeed in a system that is stacked against them, then we must provide alternative mechanisms for obtaining the necessary funding.

- All businesses ought to have a broad portfolio, because there are risks attached to putting all of their eggs in one basket. We need to help them do business in both the public and private sectors, if they are capable of serving broad markets. Most MBEs concentrate their efforts on one sector simply because they do not know enough about their alternatives.

- Public policy was most favorable to minority inclusion during the Nixon administration. Political support has declined since, especially during the last two decades. *The interests of minorities and women—and veterans—are aligned, yet their combined political influence remains dormant.* Isolated voices can be ignored, but a strong chorus will reverberate throughout Washington and every state capitol. The choir members are out there, in need of a score and a conductor.

- Opportunities are out there. So are the MBEs with the potential to be good suppliers and valuable strategic allies. The matchmaking function involves bringing people together who ought to be doing business with each other. Yet few of the nation's diverse businesses ever get helped by matchmaking in its present form.

The different functions we have just suggested are not exhaustive, and readers are encouraged to amend the categories or add their own rows to Table 6.1. But it is vital to take the next step in the analysis and assess who is doing what in each of these areas.

We have suggested some key providers in the vertical columns. Let us summarize their primary contributions:

- The SBA provides services to small businesses. Its major focus is on start-ups and early-stage businesses, but it provides some access to capital, primarily through loan guarantees, and some access to government contracts, primarily through its 8(a) program. Overall, there is little collaboration.

- The MBDA is much smaller and focuses on established minority businesses with high growth potential. It does some matchmaking. It is starved for resources. Overall, there is little collaboration.

- The support organizations serve the narrow niches specified in their mission statements. Overall, there is little collaboration.

- The advocacy organizations are all small and underfunded. None of them has a strong enough voice to significantly shape public policy. Overall, there is little collaboration.

- The political entities could have enormous influence if they had a strong focus on diverse inclusion and coordinated their efforts. Overall, there is little collaboration.

- The nation's business schools could be an agent of change, but the enormous demographic shifts are "not on the radar screen" of most, despite their urban locations. Overall, there is little collaboration.

The reader is encouraged to take out a pencil and fill in the cells in Table 6.1, rating the adequacy of coverage. Most people end up with a lot of blank cells. Most see that where there is a cell entry, coverage of particular functions is at best marginal, and even *that* assessment requires giving the benefit of the doubt.

If readers had filled in Table 6.1 twenty years ago and filled it in again today, they would not see a lot of difference. We are still seeing the same people, the same approaches, and the same results. We have not advanced very far since the 1980s, even though the world around us has changed immensely since that era.

We are not going to get better results without strong leadership. Nobody is providing the thought leadership, the policy directions, and the focus on impact. Nobody is the spokesperson for minority economic inclusion. Nobody is advocating a National Industrial Strategy that would spur the development of the national workforce and create self-sustaining local economies. And nobody is facilitating the integration of diverse efforts and ensuring that the gaps get filled.

It is a tragedy that the effort to foster minority inclusion remains so badly fractured. No leader is addressing the total problem, and some facets are not being addressed at all. This makes it all the more ironic that some entities are so engrossed in turf battles that they have little energy left for making a difference within their primary domain.

Leadership is vitally important, because we need to coordinate the whole system. Think about it. We need someone in charge of construction management if we are going to build a school. We need an experienced disaster-recovery administrator with contingency plans already drawn up to deal with the aftermath of a hurricane. And we need a joint chief of staff with a comprehensive strategy that includes roles for the army, the air force, the navy, the marines, and the intelligence community if we are going to win a war.

MINORITY BUSINESS SUCCESS REQUIRES A DIFFERENT PARADIGM

The aforementioned ten recommendations, if adopted, would generate a new paradigm for fostering the inclusion of minorities in the U.S. economy. Fresh thinking is needed, because the approaches we have been relying on until now have yielded as much benefit as we are ever likely to see. We cannot keep doing the same thing and expect different results. And we do need different results.

Strong leadership will be required to overcome resistance from those who have a vested interest in the status quo. Their unwillingness to welcome the needed change is understandable. They know how to hit targets using the old metrics. They have a comfortable role and plenty of friends in the traditional supplier diversity establishment. The circuit of events, however boring it can be at times, follows a routine that has become a comfortable part of the job. Embracing a new paradigm means giving up the familiar and taking on a challenge.

But we cannot ignore the challenge. Too much is at stake if the supplier diversity movement does not progress from where it is today to where it needs to be tomorrow. Too many good people are working hard without a strong sense of direction, and without much hope of making a real difference.

The window of opportunity is open. A new generation of leadership needs to honor what has brought us to where we are today and then take us to where we need to be tomorrow. We *must* create a different future for minorities in the U.S. economy.

Minority business success is a national priority.

NOTES

CHAPTER 1

1. Jennifer M. Ortman and Christine E. Guarneri, "United States Population Projections: 2000 to 2050" (Washington, DC: U.S. Census Bureau, 2009). Note that the percentages reflect the conservative assumption of the Low Net International Migration Series. Also note that the category Native Americans includes American Indian, Alaska Native, Native Hawaiian, and Other Pacific Islander.

2. Robert W. Fairlie and Alicia M. Robb, *Race and Entrepreneurial Success: Black-, Asian-, and White-Owned Businesses in the United States* (Cambridge, MA: The MIT Press, 2008).

3. Anthony S. Velocci Jr., "Brain Drain Threatens Aerospace Vitality," *Aviation Week & Space Technology* (April 24, 2000, p. 24). For example, the undersupply of knowledge workers has long been recognized as an industry-threatening issue in the aerospace industry, which is vital for U.S. national competitive advantage.

4. U.S. Department of Labor, *Labor Force Statistics from the Current Population Survey, Chart 2-4* (Washington, DC: U.S. Bureau of Labor Statistics, 2006), http://www.bls.gov/cps/labor2006/home.htm#education (accessed April 27, 2010).

5. Timothy Bates, *Race, Self-Employment, and Upward Mobility: An Illusive American Dream* (Washington, DC, and Baltimore, MD: Woodrow Wilson Center Press and Johns Hopkins University Press, 2007).

6. U.S. Census Bureau, *Families and Living Arrangements* (2005), http:/// www.census.gov/population/www/socdemo/hh-fam.html#history (accessed April 27, 2010.).

7. David G. Blanchflower, P. Levine, and D. Zimmerman, "Discrimination in the Small Business Credit Market," *Review of Economics and Statistics* 85, no. 4 (2003).

8. Leonard Greenhalgh and Michael Bolger, *A Different Future for Minorities in the U.S. Economy* (Hanover, NH: Tuck School of Business at Dartmouth, 2006).

CHAPTER 2

1. The Tuck School of Business at Dartmouth was established in 1900 as the nation's first graduate school of business. In 1980, it pioneered intensive learning experiences tailored to the needs of minority businesses, and today it operates the world's largest program to help minority, Native American, and women business owners. The school routinely collects data on the strengths and weaknesses of the diverse businesses it serves, creating a database involving thousands of participating MBEs. Those data show patterns that enable us to identify the most typical weaknesses of MBEs.

2. U.S. Department of Commerce, Minority Business Development Agency, *Increasing Competitive Advantage through Strategic Alliances: The Opportunity for MBEs*. August 2008.

3. An "IDIQ contract" is one that allows for indefinite delivery/indefinite quantity. This form of contract arises from the Federal Acquisition Regulation (FAR) Section 16.501(a). The time period is usually fixed, with optional time extensions. Price is usually specified, along with anticipated minimum and maximum quantities.

4. Arthur L. Stinchcombe, "Social Structure and Organizations," in *Handbook of Organizations*, ed. J. G. March, 142–193 (Chicago, IL: Rand McNally, 1965).

5. U.S. Department of Commerce, Minority Business Development Agency, *Accelerating Job Creation and Economic Productivity* (Washington, DC: 2004).

CHAPTER 3

1. There is a good precedent for this. The U.S. Department of Defense has a defense industrial strategy that specifies what industrial capacity needs to be in place to sustain the nation's military capabilities. The U.S. Department of Commerce needs to have an analogous National Industrial Strategy that specifies what industrial capacity needs to be in place to sustain the U.S. economy in a global competitive environment, and it needs to take into account the impact of changing demographics.

2. The source for Figure 3.1 is Amy E. Knaup and Merissa C. Piazza, "Business Employment Dynamics Data: Survival and Longevity, II," *Monthly Labor Review* (September 2007): 7.

3. U.S. Census Bureau, *Families and Living, Arrangements*, 2005. http:///www .census.gov/population/www/socdemo/hh-fam.html#history (accessed April 27, 2010).

4. Blanchflower, David G., P. Levine, and D. Zimmerman. 2003. "Discrimination in the Small Business Credit Market." *Review of Economics and Statistics* 85(4) (November): 930–943.

5. See, for example, *The Economist* (January 2, 2010, p.7).

CHAPTER 4

1. Time-to-market is financially and strategically important for many pharmaceutical compounds. New compounds are patented, which means competitors cannot market an identical compound throughout the lifetime of the patent, and during that time, the pharmaceutical company is free to charge whatever the market will bear. But the patent only lasts twenty years after the drug is first invented. Therefore, a year lost in the development process means a year of lost sales at high profit margins. Typically, pharmaceutical companies lose about 80 percent of the brand-name sales when generic drugs enter the market.

2. Note that the U.S. federal government has a different motivational structure for insisting that prime contractors place subcontract work with Native Americans. Indian reservations are sovereign nations located within the United States. The United States took sovereign lands away from the inhabitants some time ago and has treaties with these nations that involve compensation for the seized territories. Because the reasons for requiring outsourcing to American Indians may be different from the public-interest motives underlying outsourcing requirements for minorities and women, there is no logical basis for requiring parity between the programs. It is not unfair—as some allege, quite vehemently—for the terms of *public-interest* programs to be different from the terms of *compensation* programs. Equity does not require equality.

3. There is a temptation to pass judgment on the already privileged who want to hold on to their advantages as incumbents. But before doing so, we should be aware of the cognitive biases that shape human thinking. People tend to attribute success to their own "merit" and attribute failure to external factors, such as bad luck, an unfavorable situation, cheating by competitors, and so on. Thus it is natural for incumbents—those who already hold contracts—to believe they have a right to keep the contracts because of superior merit. It is also natural for the government—and, of course, minority business owners—to focus on its own disadvantage rather than on incumbents' merit.

This nation's history of discrimination against minorities cannot be credibly disputed and has resulted in MBEs being denied the opportunity to establish a track record of reliable performance, to rise up the learning curve, and to accumulate capital. This leads minority business owners—and some of their advocates—to dismiss the merit explanation because the playing field was never level.

As a result of these cognitive processes, there will always be some people who see set-asides as fair and others who see them as unfair. It is therefore important for public officials to articulate a clear and strong case for why inclusion mandates serve the public interest.

4. See, for example, the discussion of relationship strength, or "guanxi," in George T. Haley, Usha C. V. Haley, and Chin Tiong Tan, *The Chinese Tao of Business: The Logic of Chinese Business Strategy* (New York: Wiley, 2006).

5. For a summary of these effects, see Leonard Greenhalgh, and Zehava Rosenblatt, "Evolution of Research on Job Insecurity," *International Studies in Management and Organization* 40, no. 1 (Spring 2010): 6–15.

6. The term "bottom line" refers to the bottom line in a business's income statement (also known as "the profit and loss statement"), which shows net profit.

7. See, for example, Andrew W. Savitz and Karl Weber, *The Triple Bottom Line: How Today's Best-Run Companies Are Achieving Economic, Social, and Environmental Success, and How You Can, Too* (San Francisco: Jossey-Bass, 2006).

8. See, for example, Karen G. Mills, Elisabeth B. Reynolds, and Andrew Reamer, "Clusters and Competitiveness: A New Federal Role for Stimulating Regional Economies" (Washington, DC: Brookings Institution, 2008), http://www.brookings.edu/reports/2008/~/media/Files/rc/papers/2008/04_competitiveness reamer/Clusters%20Brief.pdf (accessed April 27, 2010). Note that Karen Mills was appointed by President Barack Obama to head the Small Business Administration.

9. U.S. Department of Commerce, Minority Business Development Agency, *Accelerating Job Creation and Economic Productivity* (Washington, DC: U.S. Department of Commerce, 2002).

CHAPTER 5

1. Colloquially, we say a socially unacceptable remark is "not politically correct."

2. The "Iron Law of Oligarchy" was first defined by German sociologist Robert Michels (1876–1936). This concept refers to the inherent tendency of all complex organizations, including populist and egalitarian institutions, to develop a ruling clique of leaders with interests in the organization itself rather than in its official aims.

3. To put the extent of coverage in perspective, the NMSDC, the largest support organization serving MBEs, has certified approximately 16,000 MBEs out of the nation's total of 4.1 million MBEs. This is less than half a percent of the minority businesses. The Women's Business Enterprise National Council (NMSDC), the largest support organization serving WBEs, has certified approximately 9,000 WBEs out of a total of 8 million WBEs. This is close to 1/10 of 1 percent of the women-owned businesses in the nation.

4. See, for example, Sydney Finkelstein, *Why Smart Executives Fail* (New York: Penguin, 2003), or Max H. Bazerman, *Judgment in Managerial Decision Making* (New York: Wiley, 1994).

5. Note that the persuasive business case for a B2B (business-to-business) corporation is different from the business case for a B2C (business-to-consumer) corporation.

6. It is important for everyone to remember that *the core mission* is not determined by who supplies the funding.

7. The challenge can be greater if the owner is Native American but not currently an enrolled member of a tribe, however, that is a complex topic that is beyond the scope of this book.

8. For example, construction, aerospace, pharmaceuticals, and automotive are very different value chains, with very different requirements.

CHAPTER 6

1. Examples of sectoral economies might include the manufacturing sector, the aerospace sector, the biotech sector, and so on. Each is an economic system in itself. Each depends on an industry cluster, a network of supporting entrepreneurial businesses, and an infrastructure that enables its success.

2. In Chapter 3, we noted that purchasing agents tend to be risk-averse, because taking on diverse suppliers has a downside potential but no upside potential. If purchasing agents do a good job and everything goes smoothly, then they are simply invisible. If they do a better job and deliver superior value for money, then people will give them no more recognition than a positive review at the end of the year. But if there is even a small supply disruption or quality problem, then management turns a spotlight on them, and that is how the purchasing agent gets remembered—as the person who jeopardized the smooth running of the organization. Because the cost of being wrong is high, purchasing agents have a natural tendency to stick with incumbent suppliers as long as they can.

3. Only the most sophisticated corporations make their internal training programs available to suppliers, even though the incremental cost of letting suppliers sit in on the sessions is usually negligible.

4. It seems ironic that the most vehement opponents of these programs tend to be equally opposed to taxation. Having all of the citizenry earning money and contributing to the tax base provides the opportunity to reduce the tax rate; conversely, keeping people on welfare in its various forms increases taxes. One would think that people who did not like paying taxes would be avid proponents of giving people who are on the sidelines today the opportunity to become economically self-sufficient tomorrow.

5. The retirement of the baby boomers—predominantly white males—will create increasing urgency for inclusion of minorities and women in the workforce and the entrepreneurial economy.

6. Recall from Chapter 4 that the old-school approach to assessing organizational success focused on a single bottom line that only reflected short-term profitability. In contrast, leading-edge corporations have a more sophisticated concept of what it means to be doing well as a corporation: their achievements are judged in terms of "the triple bottom line," which takes into account social and ecological performance, as well as financial performance.

acquisition, 21, 41–42
advocacy, for diverse businesses, 112,
    120–21, 127–28, 161
Alaska Natives, 71, 83
American Indians. *See* Native Americans

Billion Dollar Roundtable, 156
boards of minority firms, 100,
    109, 147
bonding, surety, 68–69, 78, 83,
    149–50
Brown, Robert J., 52, 54
Bush, George W., 54, 126, 151
business case for supplier diversity, 47–49,
    91–95, 120, 141, 146, 154, 155
business failures, 15, 19, 42, 56–57,
    69–70, 73, 78, 109
business plan, need for, 75
business schools, minority inclusion
    mission, 78, 79, 130, 138, 146, 147,
    159, 161

capacity of diverse businesses, 88, 96, 98,
    116, 121–22, 124–48. *See
    also* scale, of MBEs
capital, access to, 6, 12, 32, 42, 64–68, 76,
    81, 129, 145, 148–50, 159, 160
carbon consequences of management
    decisions, 104

cash flow problems, 24, 41, 64–65, 67, 99,
    109, 130, 148
celebratory events for diversity
    achievements, 98, 114, 118, 137, 143,
    154
certification of diverse status, 63–64, 113,
    122–124, 128, 152–53, 159n. *See
    also* front companies
civil rights movement, 2, 17, 53, 58, 112,
    114, 132–33, 136–37, 139
Clinton, William J., 54, 126
collaboration between support
    organizations, need for, 73–74, 78,
    80–85, 122, 127, 131–32, 135–37,
    161
commodity purchase items, 101, 116, 124,
    143, 153
community development. *See* urban
    strategy, U.S.
construction industry, 59–60, 68–69, 129,
    142, 149–50
contracts, access to. *See* purchasing
    processes
core mission of support organizations,
    117–20, 126
corporate citizenship, 99, 104
corporate reputation, 47, 94–95, 120,
    121, 156
credit, access to. *See* capital, access to

Dartmouth College. *See* Tuck School of
 Business at Dartmouth
demographics, 4–8, 14–16, 62, 90, 93,
 102, 110n9, 119n3, 133, 134–35,
 137, 138, 140
development of diverse businesses, 13, 46,
 69–70, 84, 87–111, 118, 121–22,
 145–48, 154
diversity-spend, 101, 113, 115–16, 119,
 143–44, 153–57

economic discrimination, 17, 53, 58, 95,
 115
economic growth engine, 72, 135
educational deficit, 6, 8–13, 69–70, 75,
 103, 128, 140, 146, 158
education and training for MBEs, 113,
 130, 146n3, 158, 159
emerging domestic markets, 93–94, 120,
 154
enforcement of inclusion mandates,
 60–62, 84–85
entrepreneurial economy, 7, 11, 70,
 72–73, 121, 138, 157
entrepreneurial personality, 19, 133,
 144
environmental responsibility, 55, 61, 91

free market system, 3
front companies, 109, 122, 152. *See also*
 certification of diverse status

GLBT (Gay, Lesbian, Bisexual and
 Transgender) market segment, 95
Globalization of supplier diversity efforts,
 119–20
growth of minority businesses, 20–21,
 24–25, 40–42, 65, 80, 96, 124, 142,
 144–45, 158

high school graduation rates, 9
hiring of minorities by MBEs, 16, 47n5,
 59, 92–93, 121, 135, 160
HUB Zones, 51, 64, 76, 113, 123, 128,
 151, 153

IBM, 91
immigrants, as U.S. minorities, 94, 155
immigration, 5, 15, 55
impact of support organizations, 114,
 115–116, 131, 137, 143–44, 153–57,
 163

industry clusters, 3, 15, 73, 83, 101n8,
 103, 115, 138, 140, 144, 151, 160
integration of intervention efforts, 73–74,
 78, 81, 82–85, 122, 127, 131–32,
 135–37, 157–63

job creation, 20, 47, 57, 61, 68, 75, 76,
 79, 93, 121, 134, 144–45, 156
joint ventures, 46

Kauffman Foundation, 147
King, Martin Luther, Jr., Rev., 136–37
knowledge economy, 9

Langston, Ronald J., 126
leadership of the supplier diversity
 movement, 114, 126, 127, 131–32,
 136–37, 139, 157, 158, 162
leadership succession, need for, 132
lobbying, adverse effects of, 3, 55, 62–63,
 77, 140
local economy, 47, 52, 59–60, 68, 75, 92,
 102, 121, 135, 140, 145, 150, 159,
 160
local supply base, 102–7

matchmaking, 113, 124–25, 129, 145,
 159
MBDA (Minority Business Development
 Agency), 52, 70, 78–83, 126, 138,
 151, 159
mentoring relationships, 13, 45–46, 69,
 81, 109, 130, 147

NAACP (National Association for the
 Advancement of Colored People), 91
national competitive advantage, 3, 6–7,
 11, 14, 16, 54, 121, 138, 139–41, 157
National Industrial Strategy, 3–4, 14, 15,
 52, 54–56, 139–40, 151, 162
national workforce, 55, 162
Native Americans, 50, 52, 71, 73, 82, 84,
 114, 123n7, 152
net worth, of minorities, 12n6, 66, 115,
 134, 138
new paradigm to foster minority business
 success, 136–63
Nixon, Richard M., 52, 53, 54, 78, 114,
 126, 138, 160
NMSDC (National Minority Supplier
 Development Council), 78, 119n3,
 123

Obama, Barack, 7, 54, 84, 138, 141
opponents of supplier diversity programs, 8, 92, 97, 115, 139, 150–51
opportunity fairs, 98, 113, 124, 129
outsourcing, costs of, 11, 15, 140, 155–56

pension plans, adequacy of, 16
pharmaceutical industry, 90
poverty cycle, 6, 9–10, 59, 133, 157
public policy, 47–48, 50–85, 116, 127, 136, 141, 145, 150–52, 159
purchasing processes, 29, 57–58, 60–62, 95–98, 113, 120, 143n2, 145–48

resistance to change in the supplier diversity movement, 110, 137, 163
reverse auctions, 95, 98, 124, 153
RFQ (request for quotation), 39, 45, 77, 95, 108, 153
role models, in minority communities, 20, 47, 59, 75, 121, 150, 156

SBA (U.S. Small Business Administration): loan guarantees, 75, 76, 78; mission, 51–52, 70–72, 74–78, 138, 151, 159; SBA 7(j) program, 70, 75; SBA 8(a) program, 47–48, 51, 76–77, 128, 139
scale, of MBEs, 20–21, 40, 43, 47, 48, 52, 79–80, 96, 144, 158
SCORE (Service Corps of Retired Executives) program, 81, 147
service-disabled veterans. See veterans
set-aside programs, 58–59, 128, 139, 150–51
social instability, 7, 59, 75–76, 82, 103, 115, 133
spin-off to a minority owner, 109
state level diverse inclusion programs, 50, 53, 64, 68, 73, 152
strategic alliances, 21, 43–47, 124, 144–45, 160

strategy, of a minority firm, 23, 27–29
supplier diversity movement, 17, 21, 90, 97–98, 136, 138, 143–44, 163
supply base consolidation, 40

technology transfer programs, 81
territoriality of support organizations, 84, 114, 123, 127, 131, 141, 162
thirty percent rule, 28–29
triple bottom line, 100n7, 108, 156n6
Tuck School of Business at Dartmouth, 23n1, 126
turf battles. See territoriality of support organizations

urban strategy, U.S., 51, 76, 84, 121, 138
U.S. Department of Agriculture, 70–71, 151
U.S. Department of Health and Human Services, 151
U.S. Department of Labor, 151
U.S. Department of the Interior, 52, 71, 82, 151–52

value chains, 7, 9, 14, 19–20, 22, 34–40, 46, 88–89, 101, 105–7, 116, 143–44, 146
veterans, 71–72, 73, 81, 84, 91, 123, 152, 160

WBENC (Women's Business Enterprise National Council), 78, 119n3, 123
weaknesses of minority businesses, 22–27, 56–57, 67
White House oversight, 51, 52, 53–54, 82, 84–85, 152
women, economic inclusion of, 12, 29, 62, 63, 66, 68, 72, 81, 83, 84, 93, 114, 117, 123, 136, 137, 138, 148, 151, 158, 160
workforce diversity, 92